T016676

KT-548-129

W X

Make Your Healthcare Organisation a

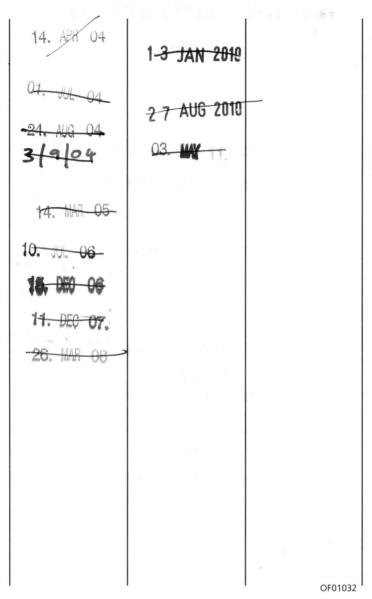

14. APR 04

07. JUL 04

24. AUG 04

3/9/04

14. MAR 05

10. JUL 06

15. DEC 06

11. DEC 07.

26. MAR 08

1 3 JAN 2010

2 7 AUG 2010

03. MAY 11

OF01032

Books should be returned to the SDH Library on or before
the date stamped above unless a renewal has been arranged

Salisbury District Hospital Library

Telephone: Salisbury (01722) 336262 extn. 4432 / 33

Out of hours answer machine in operation

Radcliffe Medical Press Ltd
18 Marcham Road
Abingdon
Oxon OX14 1AA
United Kingdom

www.radcliffe-oxford.com
The Radcliffe Medical Press electronic catalogue and online ordering facility.
Direct sales to anywhere in the world.

———————————————————————

© 2003 Wendy Garcarz, Ruth Chambers and Simon Ellis

All rights reserved. No part of this publication may be reproduced, stored in a retrieval system
or transmitted, in any form or by any means, electronic, mechanical, photocopying,
recording or otherwise without the prior permission of the copyright owner.

British Library Cataloguing in Publication Data

A catalogue record for this book is available from the British Library.

ISBN 1 85775 988 5

Typeset by Advance Typesetting Ltd, Oxfordshire
Printed and bound by TJ International Ltd, Padstow, Cornwall

Contents

Foreword

The National Health Service is in the midst of revolutionary change. If health-care professionals and organisations are going to deliver the improvements we all want to see, then healthcare organisations have to learn and develop, and support their staff. This book will help organisations to change and to do this systematically. The book includes lots of practical ways of helping organisations look at themselves, plan and implement change. It will also be helpful to anyone with lead responsibilities for learning and development, and for individuals to dip into when planning their own learning journey.

At the heart of this book is a set of values that says that people are important, that people can be responsible and do want to learn. The important people it particularly addresses are staff and service users. The prime focus is staff, but the belief that improving, supporting and developing staff makes for better experiences – and in the end probably cheaper healthcare – is a vital underpinning message.

I recommend this book as being most suitable for:

- those in trusts who have responsibility for organisational and personal development
- staff who wish to access development opportunities
- Workforce Development Confederations who need to understand how CPD money can be spent wisely and productively
- users and carers who might be interested to see how well the NHS is trying to support its staff to deliver the very highest quality of care.

I am sure that you will all find it interesting and useful.

Jan Nasir
Director of Workforce Development
Shropshire and Staffordshire Workforce
Development Confederation
May 2003

Foreword

The NHS, perhaps more than most organisations given its scale and complexity, is constantly managing changes of many types: changes in the relationship between practitioners and their patients or clients; changes between health and social care organisations and their local communities; the impact of technological change and the growth in the evidence base on health and social care interventions; changes in the nature of the workforce, as new roles develop and responsibilities shift within clinical teams; organisational changes as new organisations develop within both health and social care, often blurring established boundaries.

To maximise the opportunities for quality improvement which these changes offer, we need dynamic and vibrant organisations which can seek out the requisite knowledge and embrace change positively, to transform their patients', clients' and local communities' experiences of health and social care.

The concept of the learning organisation, which draws on research-based evidence and invests in the life-long learning and professional development of its workforce, is key to the positive management of change and to the quality improvement of services. The NHS invests over £3.5 billion in the learning of its workforce, and over £0.5 billion in research and development each year. The fruits of this investment will only be maximised, however, if organisations as a whole are committed to learning and the application of evidence. This is why *Working Together – Learning Together*, the framework for life-long learning in the NHS, required all NHS employers to have learning strategies in place by July 2002. It is also why the Government is committed to developing the proposed NHS University.

Make Your Healthcare Organisation a Learning Organisation by Wendy Garcarz, Ruth Chambers and Simon Ellis is an excellent practical guide, addressing the steps involved in developing a learning organisation and culture. It will help to translate aspirations into reality and demonstrates the importance of linking investments in individuals' learning to a learning strategy for the whole organisation.

Sir Liam Donaldson
Chief Medical Officer for England
May 2003

Preface

As authors we share the belief that there is massive underdeveloped potential within healthcare organisations, and that the organisational model of a learning organisation can provide the key to releasing that potential.

Although *learning organisations* have been discussed for more than a decade there are still sectors within the NHS that remain ignorant of the potential that they contain. This book explores the place of learning organisations in the NHS. It offers practical tools and exercises that can help to foster a positive learning culture in the NHS underpinned by the philosophy of lifelong learning.

The NHS is beginning to reap the benefits of working in multidisciplinary teams and flexible networks that encourage mutual questioning and exploration. Old-style hierarchies are proving too rigid to provide integrated service working in fast-paced, changing environments. Old-style structures do not recognise experience sufficiently, but see it as fixed, limiting and not part of developmental practice. Learning organisations recognise the value of integrating theory, practice and experience and use the three strands to challenge norms and create new views of old problems.

As healthcare moves into an era of partnership and collaboration to deliver patient-focused services, its workforce should develop an open approach to learning. Patient care should be recognised as the highest priority across organisations' boundaries whether or not they are healthcare, social care, voluntary or private sector organisations. This approach enables a wide range of views and experience from all types of professionals (clinical and non-clinical) to be considered. The learning from immediate problems and the subsequent process can then be shared across all health settings and non-health interfaces.

Transforming NHS organisations into learning organisations will require a cultural shift, adopting the philosophy and structures we have outlined above. The concept of a learning organisation is not about education and training alone. It is about developing and utilising the skills, knowledge and abilities of all its employees to ensure optimum performance, while at the same time making life rewarding and fulfilling for individuals.

A culture that values learning and the ongoing development of staff will ensure that services continue to meet the needs of patients, new service developments and policy changes. Learning should become a process of continual improvement and innovation – an ongoing cycle of action and reflection. It is important that organisations recognise and value the true contribution of lifelong learning in the achievement of their goals and objectives.

We offer you an opportunity to reflect on your culture, structures and learning practice in this book, whether you are a healthcare organisation, a healthcare team or an individual practitioner. This should provide you with a clear picture of how you operate in the current environment and how you can adapt aspects of the learning organisation culture to improve your effectiveness.

Everyone has a part to play in creating a learning organisation, however senior or influential you are in your own work setting. You might be a clinician who can influence colleagues in your team at your workplace, or a practice manager who can create a learning culture for the non-clinical support staff. You might be a training and development manager in a hospital or primary care trust who can interpret the NHS requirements and learning resources in a way that benefits the whole workforce, or you may be in an influential position to lobby for the trust's steady conversion to a learning culture. You might be a member of the trust board and in a position to shift to a more positive learning environment where the good practice described in this book is actively promoted and funded.

We have referred to the NHS structures and legislation in England for simplicity, but the whole content and ethos of this book applies just as much to healthcare organisations in any other country in the UK and beyond.

Chapters 1 and 2 will give you some basic explanations and context to lifelong learning and developing learning cultures within organisations.

Chapters 3 and 4 focus on what you can do to establish a philosophy and culture of learning and how these directly influence the quality of performance and service delivery using national directives as a vehicle.

Chapter 5 is full of practical tools and exercises to help the NHS workforce at all levels to move their organisation towards a learning culture. The practicalities of developing learning organisations requires their leadership and management teams to undertake specific exercises to set the process of creating a learning culture in motion.

Chapters 6 and 7 give you practical guidance about how to tailor the tools and concepts to your healthcare organisation, whether it is within the primary or secondary care sector.

Chapter 8 explores the roles of the patient as a learner, teacher and performance monitor in a modernised NHS.

Chapter 9 draws some conclusions and offers several templates to get you started on an action plan for putting some of the ideas and suggestions in this book into practice.

Wendy Garcarz
Ruth Chambers
Simon Ellis
May 2003

About the authors

Wendy Garcarz is an education and development specialist with a proven record of accomplishment in primary care. She has 20 years' experience in education and training management in both the public and private sectors. She has spent the last 12 years working in primary care, developing primary care clinicians and support workers in service commissioning, continuing professional development, strategic planning and service innovations. Wendy is the managing director of *4-health Ltd*, an organisational development consultancy specialising in sustainable change through workforce investment. She works with all types of healthcare organisation and can be contacted via www.4-health.biz.

Ruth Chambers has been a GP for 20 years. Her previous experience has encompassed a wide range of research and educational activities, including stress and the health of doctors, the quality of healthcare, healthy working, the care of prisoners, teenagers' contraception and many other topics. She is currently a part-time GP, the Professor of Primary Care Development at Staffordshire University, the national education lead for the NHS Alliance and Head of the Teaching PCT programme in North Staffordshire. Ruth was the national convenor for Accredited Professional Development (APD) for the Royal College of General Practitioners. She was the Chairman of Staffordshire Medical Audit Advisory Group and a GP trainer.

Simon Ellis is a consultant neurologist and Clinical Director of the Neurosciences Department at North Staffordshire Hospital. He is a visiting professor in Neurosciences at Staffordshire University. He is also the Director of the senior house officer (SHO) rotation in general (internal) medicine at North Staffordshire Hospital. Simon has a day-to-day commitment to educating healthcare staff and runs small groups on communication skills as well as more formal lectures on neurological topics. He has direct educational supervisory responsibility for the medical SHOs at North Staffordshire Hospital. He is also responsible for consultant appraisal within the Neurosciences Directorate.

Acknowledgements

Staffordshire University has been commissioned by Shropshire and Staffordshire Workforce Development Confederation to lead an initiative to encourage a shift in the culture of local hospital and primary care trusts to that of *learning organisations*. This book has been developed from the initiative and the associated publications with contributions from Ann Fisher:

- Fisher A, Garcarz W, Chambers R *et al.* (2002) *Towards a Learning Organisation. A strategy for healthcare organisations.* Staffordshire University, Stoke-on-Trent.
- Garcarz W, Fisher A, Chambers R *et al.* (2003) *Towards a Learning Organisation. Organisational development toolkits.* Staffordshire University, Stoke-on-Trent.

Both of these publications are reproduced on the West Midlands deanery website: http://www.wmdeanery.org.

We should like to acknowledge the fantastic help and support of Barbara Brown in preparing the final manuscript.

Glossary

AHP	Allied Health Professions
ALS	Action Learning Set
APD	Accredited Professional Development
BMA	British Medical Association
BS	British Standard
CATS	Credit Accumulation and Transfer Scheme
CCST	Certificate of Completion of Specialist Training
CHAI	Commission for Healthcare Audit and Inspection
CHI	Commission for Health Improvement
CNST	Clinical Negligence Scheme for Trusts
CPD	Continuing Professional Development
CSP	Chartered Society of Physiotherapy
DoH	Department of Health
ECDL	European Computer Driving Licence
EFQM	European Foundation for Quality Management
FBA	Fellowship by Assessment
FE	Further Education
GMC	General Medical Council
GP	General Practitioner
GPC	General Practitioners Committee
GPwSI	General Practitioner with Special Interest
HE	Higher Education
HEFCE	Higher Education Funding Council for England
HPC	Health Professions Council
IIP	Investors in People
ISO	International Organisation for Standardisation
IT	Information Technology
LMCA	Long-term Medical Conditions Alliance
MAP	Membership by Assessment of Performance
MRCP	Membership of the Royal College of Physicians
NAO	National Audit Office
NHDU	Neurosciences High Dependency Unit
NHS	National Health Service
NHSIA	NHS Information Authority
NHSU	NHS University
NMC	Nursing and Midwifery Council
NSF	National Service Framework
NVQ	National Vocational Qualification

PCG   Primary Care Group
PCO   Primary Care Organisation
PCT   Primary Care Trust
PEST   Political Economic Sociological Technological
PREP   Post-registration Education and Practice
QTD   Quality Team Development
R&D   Research and Development
RCGP   Royal College of General Practitioners
REC   Research Ethics Committee
SHO   Senior House Officer
SpR   Specialist Registrar
SHA   Strategic Health Authority
SWOT   Strengths Weaknesses Opportunities Threats
TQM   Total Quality Management
UKCC   United Kingdom Central Council for Nursing
WDC   Workforce Development Confederation
WTE   Whole Time Equivalent

1

What is a learning organisation?

The basic definition of a learning organisation is: 'An organisation that is continually expanding its capacity to create its own future.'[1] A learning organisation focuses on continually expanding people's capacity and nurturing new ways of thinking. It incorporates systems thinking, personal mastery, shared vision and team learning.

'A learning organisation facilitates the learning of all its members and consciously transforms itself ... contributing to the learning of the wider community or context of which it is a part.'[2] For such organisations it is not enough to practise 'survival learning' in order to just keep pace with change. They need to practise 'creation learning' that enables the organisation to ride the wave of change through innovation, developing new ways of working and problem solving.

Essentially, learning organisations are visions of what corporate structures can deliver when they recognise the value and contribution of their workforce through lifelong learning. They are fundamentally different in structure from ordinary organisations, in that education and training forms a central plank of corporate strategy, which informs strategic planning, workforce planning, risk management and performance review functions. This can be a difficult concept to come to terms with, as financial capability and performance targets (that are often purely quantitative) drive many traditional structures. This is diametrically opposed to the ethos of service sector organisations where qualitative measures most often define success.

The trends of modern leadership and management are quickly moving away from old-style 'command and control' models and are embracing empowerment, shared responsibility and skill/knowledge development. This gives organisations the competitive edge to retain the talented and skilled elements of their workforce.

Motivation and morale are easier to maintain, and performance tends to be consistently higher in these types of learning organisations. An innovative workforce is able to spot trends and operate ahead of change, creating flexibility and responsiveness – and effectively change-proofing the organisation.

A learning organisation is commonly found in fast-moving, change-prone environments, where organisations need to be flexible to meet their customers' demands and where external forces such as legislation change the expectations and objectives of the organisation, usually at very short notice.

The battle cry of resource-stretched organisations is 'we need to work smarter not harder', but this requires creative thinking by senior management teams, and the inclusion and empowerment of the whole workforce so that 100% of effort is channelled towards organisational objectives. The difficulty is that people need a clear picture of the organisation's ultimate goals if they are to understand the importance of their contributions.

Learning organisations are very good at painting a clear picture of their ultimate goals or their vision, and sharing them with the whole workforce so that all staff members feel a part of the achievement of their common goals. Learning organisations also realise that the workforce cannot be expected to perform in such a complex environment without developing their capabilities along the way. This sort of environment breeds organisational change, and wherever that exists, training and education needs are met. The very nature of a learning organisation recognises this pattern and ensures that the values, processes and mechanisms exist to enable individual staff members to learn throughout their work lifespan, to keep pace with change, and continually improve their performance and the organisation's effectiveness.

What is a learning organisation?

A learning organisation is one that recognises that the whole workforce needs opportunities to learn new skills and knowledge and apply those in their working environment in order to keep pace with change and maintain organisational effectiveness. This is particularly important as organisations become 'leaner' and 'flatter', trimming their management hierarchy. The workforce needs to be multiskilled from the domestic/support staff, to clinicians and allied health professionals, right up to senior management and the organisation's leaders.

Learning organisations should view their workforce through a range of assumptions:

- Lifelong learning is key to supporting the acquisition and application of new skills and knowledge.
- The motivational aspects of learning improve morale and individual performance.
- People are generally resourceful and want to do well in their jobs.

A learning organisation is one that practically displays its support and commitment for lifelong learning by:

- ensuring that education, training and development are central planks of corporate strategy

- producing a statement of intent that formalises the organisation's commitment to lifelong learning
- ensuring that the whole workforce have feedback on their performance (usually through individuals' appraisals or performance review) and access to a needs analysis process in order to produce annual personal development/learning plans
- evaluating and reflecting on the learning that takes place in order to repeat what works and change what does not, and in turn achieve corporate objectives.

A significant overhaul of the education and learning philosophy/strategy and priorities is required to deliver this level of organisational change. That means developing a different view of the place of learning cultures in healthcare organisations.

Where does lifelong learning fit in?

Lifelong learning is simply the recognition of people's need to continually learn new skills, take on new knowledge and develop new behaviours and attitudes throughout their life, from 'cradle to grave'. Its foundation stone is one of opportunity, ensuring that when individuals are ready to learn, the opportunity is afforded them to do so. In reality an individual's pattern of learning may not be consistent. It will have gaps and rest periods but a general momentum will be evident. In a world such as the NHS where change is increasing in its velocity, it is realistic to expect learning to have a 'shelf life' i.e. the time that elapses before information or skills are out of date. In most sectors the learning shelf life is geared to the pace of change – so, in healthcare, shelf life varies from 12 months to 3 years depending on the particular topic. In the field of information technology, the shelf life is even less, being approximately 6 to 18 months.

Most organisations, including the NHS, have their share of reluctant learners. The profile of these individuals will include very experienced staff members with long service records, people who are considering retirement or those who are not ambitious and are satisfied with their current role or level of responsibility. The challenge is to engage these individuals, as their contribution in the changing environment, such as that in healthcare, is important to overall effectiveness. The mind shift required by reluctant learners is to accept that learning is inherent to their role and not an optional extra.

Lifelong learning is the cornerstone of a learning organisation that ensures that all of its workforce have fair access to learning opportunities, processes that review performance and identifies their learning needs. Subsequently, individuals and teams should be given support to achieve their potential. The learner is recognised as significant in these organisations as he/she gains the knowledge and skills that enable the organisation to achieve its objectives.

The evidence of lifelong learning within an organisation is to be found in the levels at which learning takes place and the infrastructure that delivers learning opportunities. Box 1.1 outlines the key elements that constitute a lifelong learning culture, demonstrating the learning philosophy, the quality measures and the infrastructure requirements.

Box 1.1:   Elements of a lifelong learning culture

- **Ethical learning:** evidence of organisational commitment for professional and personal learning; learning that is part of the quality improvement cycle; patient participation programmes; and learning through reflection, risk management and complaints processes.
- **Empirical learning:** learning through experience; learning that takes place throughout the lifespan of employees, policies and systems, in planned and intentional ways.
- **Partnership learning:** evidence of cross-boundary learning with other organisations, professions, education providers, academic institutions and related sector organisations.
- **A set of core values:** behaviours, symbols and rituals that promote learning opportunities for all.
- **A set of standards:** common standards, rewards and sanctions that recognise good practice, define poor practice and apply those standards right across the organisation in a meaningful way.
- **A mechanism for defining expectations:** expectations of the learner by the organisation, and vice versa.
- **A process for systematic reflection:** review that continually improves the effectiveness of the organisation's and the individual's abilities to learn.

Ethical learning is usually represented by a statement of intent issued by the organisation which clearly outlines the organisation's values around learning opportunity and the importance it has as a strategic tool contributing to overall performance and effectiveness. It demonstrates the way in which learning links key operational tasks and priorities together, providing a whole-systems approach to planning, service configuration and performance measurement. In effect, it outlines the organisation's learning philosophy.

Empirical learning illustrates the management's commitment to planned and intentional learning through the policies and procedures that the organisation has in place. It removes the barriers which may exist concerning fair access, protected time, systematic needs identification and reflective practice, and smooths the way for learning opportunities to be created for the whole workforce (in an appropriate format). It openly values the learning that comes directly from good practice and systematises dissemination of that learning.

Partnership learning recognises the value of cross-boundary, cross-cultural learning that can take place between partner organisations. In complex environments where professions, organisations and public, voluntary and private sector organisations work together, the obvious approach is also to learn together.

A set of core values establishes the principles of learning which guide the organisation. It also sets out custom and practice and the behaviours that display those values in everyday working. These values are important to the individuals within the organisation as they validate their learning experiences.

A set of standards offers a benchmark for good learning practice and also establishes the conditions of application. Standards mean very little unless people are clear about the benefits of adhering to them and the consequences of ignoring them. The standards may be created by the organisation but they will probably be influenced by external factors. For example, a healthcare organisation in England may produce a set of standards that reflects the nurse education strategy derived by the local Workforce Development Confederation (WDC) but the consequences of not applying those standards may result in a nurse failing the registration process of the Nursing and Midwifery Council (NMC).

A mechanism for defining expectations of both the organisation and individual learners ensures that the policies, education and training provision and learning methods are operating effectively. This regular, two-way communication can be achieved through the evaluation process, through a specialised education and training group that shapes policy or through the performance review process.

A process for systematic reflection ensures that individuals have the opportunity to identify what learning works, improve their practice and realise what is not effective. This method of continuous improvement ensures the transfer of learning from formal situations directly into everyday practice. It can also benefit the wider organisation by tackling problematic areas of operation through risk management processes, significant event analysis and learning sets. This internally generated, problem-solving approach is widely recognised as the most effective way of ensuring consistent service quality.

When viewed holistically, these elements of a learning culture set out a clear plan of key issues that can support the transition of a traditional organisational culture towards the development of a learning organisation.

Continuing professional development (CPD) in a learning organisation

Many professions are becoming self-regulated and as a result the emphasis on professional capability rests with individuals. Evidence that professionals regularly update their skills and knowledge to keep pace with change is required to satisfy professional standards, maintain public and clientele confidence and minimise the risks of poor practice and adverse events.

Learning organisations take a much broader view of the CPD process and actively use it as a quality improvement mechanism, a support for the recruitment and retention of skilled staff and a reward for individuals wanting to progress in their careers. CPD offers a ready-made framework to support educational requirements, needs identification and reinforcement of reflective practice. Good CPD practice requires individuals to take responsibility for their own learning in terms of planning and evaluation. The organisation's responsibilities are to signpost and, where appropriate, provide learning opportunities that meet individuals' requirements. The organisation should provide a supportive learning environment that allows individuals to learn and apply their learning in their work situations and to evaluate the effectiveness of the training provision. This learning partnership between organisation and learner is indicative of a learning culture where both parties take some responsibility and share the benefits.

Learning is central to organisational development and planning

In order to deliver the NHS Plan[3] and to meet the requirements of the NHS Modernisation Agency, healthcare organisations have to find ways of working differently to reflect the changing pattern of resources and current legislation. The mechanism employed to identify requirements and plan and implement change is 'organisational development'. This term covers a whole range of activities from supporting cultural change and devising corporate planning strategy to implementing appraisal and performance review systems.

> 'Organisational development is a specific methodology for effecting change to improve organisational effectiveness.'[4]

What this definition establishes is that where there is change, a mechanism for managing the new knowledge is required to capture organisational benefits. Introducing change to any organisation is a complex business but in healthcare organisations it is further complicated by the diversity of the workforce and their learning requirements to be able to keep pace with external demands.

Figure 1.1 illustrates learning as a central function of a learning organisation, feeding corporate planning and related activities, and thereby facilitating the achievement of organisational objectives. It places learning at the centre of the organisation, receiving information on corporate issues, and furnishing

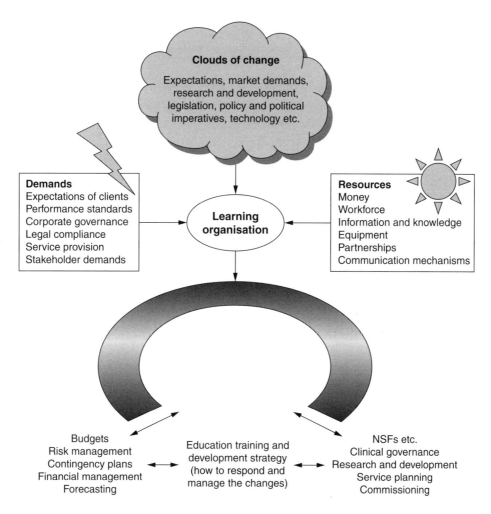

Clouds of change

Expectations, market demands, research and development, legislation, policy and political imperatives, technology etc.

Demands
Expectations of clients
Performance standards
Corporate governance
Legal compliance
Service provision
Stakeholder demands

Learning organisation

Resources
Money
Workforce
Information and knowledge
Equipment
Partnerships
Communication mechanisms

Budgets
Risk management
Contingency plans
Financial management
Forecasting

Education training and development strategy (how to respond and manage the changes)

NSFs etc.
Clinical governance
Research and development
Service planning
Commissioning

Figure 1.1: Learning as a central function in a healthcare organisation.

strategies and solutions that deliver results. In some traditional healthcare organisations the training function is seen as a practical necessity but has a low priority. Training in such organisations is viewed as a cost, not an investment, and when the organisation is placed under financial pressure it is usually the first casualty of budget cuts. The result may be quick fixes and tick boxes, but the organisation often stores up problems which are highlighted during performance reviews and audits at a later date.

Learning organisations see the learning function as their key to managing change and achieving organisational effectiveness regardless of the business climate. As the organisation is viewed as a whole system it is not possible to see things in isolation and the consequences of a single action can be clearly identified. This builds a robust corporate planning process and helps to prioritise business decisions based on likely outcomes, rather than purely bottom-line figures, which deliver sustainability, cohesion and long-term achievement of goals.

Structure of a learning organisation

The structure of a learning organisation is most easily understood when represented as three key elements.

- Philosophy and vision: the element that establishes the commitment and desire to create a learning organisation culture.
- Learning strategy: the element that implements a learning organisation culture.
- Learning mechanisms: the element that practically demonstrates a learning organisation in action.

Learning organisations operate in two environments. The first of these is the internal environment – the values, behaviours, systems and processes that define the learning culture. The second is the external environment which influences organisations in terms of legislation, national policy, other sector developments and current thinking and practice.

Figure 1.2 illustrates how these elements come together to form a learning organisation. It shows the relationship between internal and external factors and how both can influence the philosophy and values of the organisation, which in turn affects the implementation of strategy and policy and the selection and use of learning resources.

Functions of a learning organisation

The organisation's role is to develop a corporate ability to manage that knowledge and apply those skills in the most effective way. There are practical systems for gathering and organising information – libraries, databases etc. – but there also need to be frameworks that recognise less formal pathways of recognition of learning, promotion and career development that support individuals in growing and developing.

These functions fall into two categories. The first is the functionality of the organisation itself, which is to:

- deliver effective services within resource constraints and workforce capabilities
- ensure organisational rejuvenation and innovation through learning
- provide practical support and mechanisms to enable lifelong learning for all, maximising organisational effectiveness
- scan the environment constantly to spot trends and changes at the earliest opportunity, protecting the leading edge of the organisation
- enter into learning partnerships with other organisations to develop organisational capacity and capability.

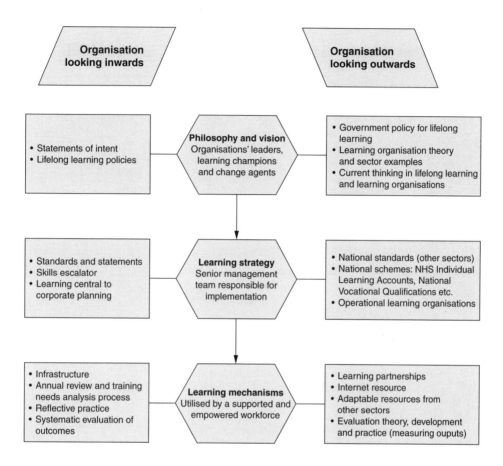

Figure 1.2: Structure of a learning organisation.

The second is the functionality of its workforce, which is to:

- provide and promote a culture that engages all, inspires learning and values learning outcomes
- evaluate systematically the value and contribution of learning at individual and organisational levels
- provide learning opportunities and resources that reflect a range of learning styles and methodologies.

These functions are not the only ones that are relevant but they are the ones with the highest priority.

The simple questionnaire which follows should enable you to see how *learning-friendly* your own organisation is. It explores elements of the culture, structure and functions of a learning organisation to help you to measure the extent to which your own organisation is a learning organisation.

How learning-friendly is your organisation?

This checklist will indicate how far your organisation has developed a learning culture. Look at each statement carefully and tick the appropriate box to indicate to what extent the statement applies to your organisation. Use the following score:

1 = Does not apply
3 = Applies to a large extent

2 = Applies somewhat
4 = Applies totally

Criteria	*Score*			
	1	**2**	**3**	**4**
1.0 Development of a learning organisation				
1.1 A vision or mission statement has been produced and disseminated throughout your organisation concerning its commitment to lifelong learning.				
1.2 There is a statement of intent linked to lifelong learning in your corporate plan.				
1.3 A set of principles or values has been produced by your organisation stating commitment to lifelong learning, education and workforce development.				
2.0 Strategy for a learning organisation				
Learning opportunities are created by:				
2.1 Empirical learning – learning that takes place through the lifespan of all employees in a planned and intentional way.				
2.2 Ethical learning – evidence of organisational support for professional and personal learning that is connected to the planning and quality improvement mechanisms.				
2.3 Partnership learning – evidence of cross-boundary learning with other organisations, professions, social care providers or voluntary sector organisations.				
3.0 Development of a learning culture				
3.1 There is an educational infrastructure (i.e. education policy, induction programmes, core training programmes, teaching facilities).				
3.2 There is a continuing professional development process available to all qualified staff (e.g. appraisal/performance review, policies for study leave and funding, minimum standards for protected learning time), a fair-access procedure open to all employees.				
3.3 Learning partnerships are evident (i.e. delivery of common training modules across boundaries, secondment and shadowing opportunities, curriculum development with further education and higher education partners).				

continued opposite

	Criteria		Score		
3.4	There are clinical priorities integrated into the learning process (e.g. critical event analysis, clinical supervision, service developments).				
3.5	There is a clear process for identifying an individual's training and development needs (i.e. an annual review and individual development/learning plan).				
3.6	There is support for undergraduate and pre-registration students (e.g. clinical placements, mentoring and supervision).				
4.0	**Implementation of a learning culture**				
4.1	There is a clear framework of professional standards and workforce training and development.				
4.2	There is a mechanism to integrate training and development and the implementation of organisational priorities, e.g. National Service Frameworks etc.				

How did your organisation score?

Scores	Conclusions
48–56	Congratulations – you are a developing learning organisation. Use the following chapters to continue to refine and maintain your learning culture.
39–47	Your organisation has made a good start but it is important to ensure that the foundation stones are in place. Robust systems are important but clear responsibilities and ownership by the workforce are just as important. Use the following chapters to identify gaps and reinforce your learning culture.
26–38	Your organisation probably has a few processes in place but may be lacking the top-level statements and cultural elements that are vital. Use the following chapters to reinforce a structured approach to developing your learning culture.
13–25	All of this is probably new to your organisation but if you work through the chapters and exercises in the book as an organisation, you can establish a learning culture.

References

1   Senge P (1990) *The Fifth Discipline.* Doubleday, New York.

2   Pedler M, Burgoyne J and Boydell T (1996) *The Learning Company.* McGraw-Hill, London.

3   Department of Health (2000) *The NHS Plan.* Department of Health, London.

4   Buchanan DA and Huczynski AA (1985) *Organisational Behaviour* (3e). Prentice Hall, London.

2

Learning philosophy in the NHS

Policy imperatives of lifelong learning and learning culture in the NHS

The NHS is a hugely complex organisation and until recently has been operated as a bureaucracy, governed by hierarchy, with rules and regulations that have largely remained unchanged for decades. The major service review and restructuring of the NHS has, however, been impeded by less than ideal conditions. As patient demand increases, fed by increasingly sophisticated access to information and internal market forces, efficiency pressures on all healthcare organisations have resulted. Fundamental questions are being posed about how the NHS is maintaining service quality through adequate resources and a properly trained and developed workforce. Low morale and difficult working conditions have created a situation where change is often viewed by the workforce with suspicion and cynicism.

When the NHS Plan[1] was launched, the associated modernisation programme was intended to update methods and practice and ensure consistent standards of patient care across the country. This has called into question the whole system of how organisations are structured and operated, how roles and responsibilities are defined and how the workforce is developed to effect the necessary changes.

The document *Working Together – Learning Together*[2] is a framework for lifelong learning in the NHS and it reinforces the message that learning and development is a key success factor in the delivery of the NHS Plan. The framework emphasises developing the whole NHS workforce and introduces the 'skills escalator' concept whereby staff are trained and skilled to the maximum of their ability irrespective of where they start in the workforce (*see* Box 2.1).

The ongoing NHS drive to improve working conditions and offer family-friendly policies to encourage the recruitment and retention of staff has established a precedent to develop and reward staff for their commitment.[3,4] The government's intention to invest in NHS staff is clear, but how this intention manifests itself is vitally important. Organisations should take responsibility for creating the right conditions and environment that inspire and engage the

---

Box 2.1:   The skills escalator[2]

With the skills escalator approach, staff are encouraged through a strategy of lifelong learning to constantly renew and extend their skills and knowledge, enabling them to move *up* the 'escalator'. Meanwhile workload should be delegated *down* the escalator.

Seven categories of staff are considered within the skills escalator.

1   Socially excluded individuals who can be placed on employment orientation programmes to develop an understanding of working life.
2   The unemployed placed in starter jobs with structured training and development.
3   Less skilled or experienced people already working within the NHS can be developed by use of job rotation and training and development programmes, in conjunction with their appraisal and personal development plans.
4   Semi-skilled workers can be developed though NVQs or equivalent vocational qualifications, to put them in a position where they can access education towards professional qualifications.
5   Qualified professionals can identify development needs and use training and job rotation opportunities to acquire a range of skills at staged intervals through the use of appraisal and development.
6   Staff in more demanding or complex posts will require support for continued learning and skills development.
7   The most advanced staff will continue to develop by means of flexible 'portfolio careers', planned in partnership with employers, informed by appraisal, career and development planning processes.

---

professions, making an NHS role something of real value. This requires a basic understanding of what motivates people to give their best performance. Box 2.2 gives an example of the planned benefits from one of the current governmental initiatives which depend on creating motivated staff.

Box 2.2:   Some of the hoped-for benefits of role redesign in primary care[4]

• Managing an ever-increasing workload – by better deployment of staff skills.
• Reduced vacancies and staff turnover – from boosting job satisfaction.
• Job satisfaction – through career development.
• Development of special interests – develop specialist interests that lead to more patients being treated in primary care.
• Reduction in patient waiting times – more efficient use of staff skills.
• More personalised care.
• A more flexible and responsive workforce – staff are more adaptable in response to patient demand.

Professionals need to keep pace with developments and therefore need genuine support to identify and meet their training needs. The current demands placed on all health and social care workers to change practices and develop new ways of working are significant. As a result, the education and training needs of clinicians, nurses, allied health professionals and support staff are changing. Leaders of NHS organisations and relevant professions need to make a direct link between policy imperatives and the delivery of better health and social care services with improved health and social outcomes for patients.

A learning culture that promotes lifelong learning is a key requirement for delivering the policy and guidance that will produce a national health service that operates well into the next century.

Learning as an organisational philosophy in the NHS

With the recent interest in learning and education, the health service has clearly stated its intention to demand genuine commitment from healthcare organisations and the professionals that work in them to develop learning cultures based on a philosophy of lifelong learning.[1,2] This commitment will require a significant overhaul of learning and educational philosophy at organisational levels.

Learning needs to be viewed as an essential activity and have a much higher profile at the trust's board level and in corporate planning meetings in order to deliver the organisational change benefits of which the healthcare organisation is capable. That means developing a different view of the place of learning cultures in healthcare organisations and an overview of the NHS learning and education infrastructure to identify what exists and to plot gaps. This could be achieved by conducting an organisational gap analysis.

Figure 2.1 identifies key organisations that have a strategic interest in education and training. The list is not exhaustive but it outlines the diversity of organisations who have a vested interest in the strategic development of education and training throughout the NHS.

The Department of Health (DoH), as a policy developer, establishes standards and outcomes and works closely with DoH directorates (policy implementers), Royal Colleges, professional bodies and special interest groups to define implementation structures and timescales. The professional bodies and associations have a less obvious role but, notwithstanding, a strategically important one. They set the professional standards and codes of conduct that govern their members' practice. This places them in a unique position to influence policy and guidance.

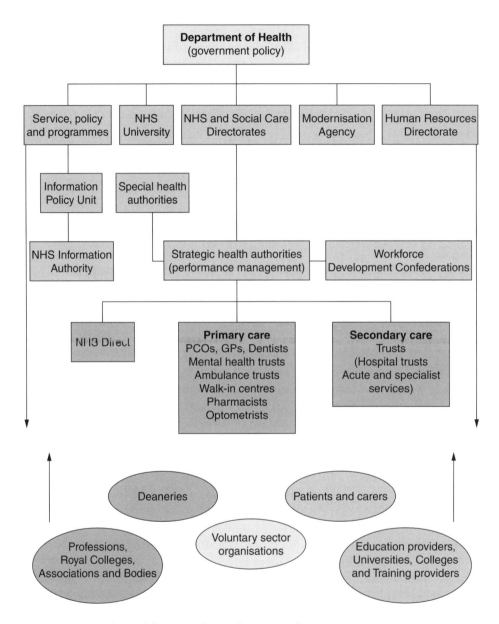

Figure 2.1: Relational diagram of NHS education and training structures.

Learning and performance monitoring

Performance monitors include the Commission for Health Improvement (CHI) and the strategic health authorities (SHAs) in England who are responsible for measuring clinical effectiveness and organisational performance. CHI will evolve into the Commission for Healthcare Audit and Inspection (CHAI) with the merger of CHI with the Audit Commission, the National Care Standards Commission and the Mental Health Act Commission. The new body will continue to emphasise the essential learning lessons to be had from its clinical governance reviews of NHS organisations in England and Wales to improve patient care (*see* Box 2.3). CHAI will inspect both NHS and private healthcare sectors to establish both the quality of patient care and how effectively resources are being used.

Box 2.3: Common emerging themes from CHI reviews of trusts (the 133 reports were mainly drawn from the secondary care sector)[5]

- Organisations are reactive rather than proactive and respond to problems as they happen rather than considering future risks and planning to prevent them from occurring.
- There is a lack of organisation-wide policies and strategies on clinical governance.
- Policies and strategies when they do exist are not implemented.
- Learning is not shared across and between organisations.
- There is a lack of communication from strategic to operational levels.
- There is a lack of sharing between different staff groups.

As the strategic health authorities develop, their activities will be more outcome driven, but in this period of establishment they may take an arbitrary measure of the published milestones set by current guidance. At first these may not be seen as part of the whole system, but simply as another 'box to be ticked'. Learning outcomes should be part of a robust evaluation rather than just acknowledging that a system has been set up.

The complex picture can generate mixed messages about the philosophy of learning across the NHS

Service deliverers are implementing policy using internal resources set against an established (or in some cases *establishing*) culture. Many of these organisations understand, to varying degrees, the importance of education and learning as a corporate effectiveness tool, but others are entrenched in traditional cultures and fail to capitalise on their development as learning organisations.

Education and training commissioners and providers occupy opposing positions in the education marketplace but should be driven by similar priorities around curriculum development, skills acquisition and knowledge management. There are many others in this category. They tend to be external organisations that provide education, such as deaneries, vocational training providers and voluntary sector organisations that work directly with healthcare professionals and support workers to offer training and development programmes.

What Figure 2.1 illustrates is the complex map of those involved in education and training with the numerous permutations of learning partnerships that can occur. Added to this, each of these organisations will have their own expectations and agendas, and will want a variety of things from education and learning.

Funding of learning in healthcare organisations

Funding issues further complicate this picture, as there are many funding streams that carry rigid regulations on how and for what the money is used. Many of these regulations were formulated prior to the modernisation programme and emphasis on lifelong learning. In response, the Department of Health in England is reviewing funding streams to reduce the complexity and bureaucracy involved.[6] This consultation document considers how the NHS should use its £3 billion annual funding for learning and personal development to support the development of staff better, and to deliver the necessary skills to support patient-centred services and public health strategies. Box 2.4 describes how the DoH proposes that funding should be reorganised on an interdisciplinary basis, ending the present rigid demarcations in the support given to different professions and occupational groups.

In England, Workforce Development Confederations (WDCs) are leading on the development of these issues. They are in a very strong position to effect real change as they can take a 'macro' view of the funding process and the anomalies and inequalities that currently exist. They also have a strategic view of NHS priorities and the education and training needs of the workforce in order to lead the workforce planning activities that ensure enough trained and competent staff are available to deliver the healthcare of the future.

Box 2.4:   Consultation on the review of NHS education and training funding[6]

The document proposes that the key values listed below should underpin future funding allocations.

- *Transparency* – education commissioners should be able to account fully for their use of funding.
- *Equity* – the main driver should be the need to deliver particular healthcare skills to patients rather than the delivery of particular types of professionals.
- *Comprehensiveness* – support should be available to all health service staff, with or without existing professional qualifications.

continued opposite

- *Responsiveness* – learning and development must be able to adapt quickly to support the delivery of new skills and new types of worker as requirements change and the workforce develops.
- *Integration* – healthcare staff of different disciplines should learn together as a precursor to, and continuing dimension of, working together.
- *Partnership* – the health and education sectors, social care, and private and voluntary sectors should work together to deliver training.
- *Flexibility* – people should be able to step on and off learning, accumulating credits.

The National Audit Office (NAO) report *Educating and Training the Future Health Professional Workforce for England*[7] considered specific issues around funding for non-medical education and training and attrition from courses and found the following.

- Many higher education institutions believed that, if they were to continue to expand student numbers, there would need to be investment in the capital infrastructure.
- The NHS did not have the information to understand or compare institutions' costing policies because some contracts between higher education institutions and consortia had clauses maintaining commercial confidentiality.
- There were wide variations in the price per student for the same qualification. Variations in the relationship between price and cost might not have led to the best allocations of resources.
- There were no common contract and standard benchmark prices and a lack of consistent benchmark standards in assuring quality.

A parallel study by the Audit Commission,[8] which considered education, training and development for healthcare staff in NHS trusts, looked at the way that trusts used their own resources and demonstrated wide variation in the management of training of staff. It found major variations – up to fivefold in spending levels between trusts – and a failure in many cases to take account of training in such developments as in the local delivery plans.

How the NHS University fits in

The formation of the NHS University (NHSU) signals commitment from the government and all levels of the NHS to provide the whole workforce with high standards of educational opportunities that reflect the changes and developments of the service. The NHSU will be available to the one million people working for the NHS from autumn 2003, including people employed by private companies providing services. Box 2.5 gives an overview of what type of learning support individuals will be offered. Learning materials will be available online and staff will be able to access them through NHS systems, cybercafés in healthcare organisations and through digital TV. It is intended that the NHSU will receive university status in time and will be able to grant its own academic awards. It will provide a core curriculum; act as a signpost to existing training; provide a range of foundation, first-line and basic training programmes; quality-assure and accredit existing training; and develop evaluation tools to ensure that education improves patient care.[9]

Box 2.5:   The NHS University pledge to individual staff working in the NHS is to:

- support them with high quality education, training and development
- bring education to the teams where they work
- encourage real learning based on clinical practice, not theory
- develop their career potential throughout their working lives.[9]

Professions may promote learning as being central to their reaccreditation or revalidation and CPD processes, with an emphasis on meeting professional standards and not necessarily making the link to organisational effectiveness.

Strategic health authorities may view learning as a component of performance review, as another milestone to measure systems and structures, and not analyse the learning outcomes and their impact on health gain.

External providers may see learning as a vehicle to promote their traditional programmes and activities and not take the opportunity to involve professional and healthcare organisations in developing a future curriculum or course content. Some service deliverers may see learners as a strategic tool to support change and improve organisational effectiveness while others may see learning as a corporate function with limited appeal and value.

New educational requirements of today's NHS

It is clear that, as a result of sector restructuring, a range of new educational requirements has been highlighted and that all organisations, groups, teams and individuals need to reflect on their own learning practices to assess how they measure up to the current education agenda, as Box 2.6 shows. All have an opportunity to influence the development of a learning culture through their activities, initiatives and evaluation processes.

The modernisation agenda has highlighted many new educational needs for all doctors, nurses, therapists, managers and support staff. Many of the new needs are centred around commissioning and delivering healthcare through newly developed roles and the increased emphasis on patient and public

---

Box 2.6: New educational requirements of today's NHS

- Education and training plans that complement those of the department, directorate or practice, of trusts and primary care organisations, district and central priorities but also reflect professional and personal development.
- The implementation of clinical governance: knowledge, positive attitudes, new skills and a learning culture.
- Adoption of evidence-based practice: where and how to get the information, how to apply the evidence and monitor changes.
- Needs assessments: how to do them, who to work with, linking needs assessment with commissioning and providing care, finding ways to reduce health inequalities.
- Training needs analysis driven by skill and knowledge requirements to improve effectiveness, and not driven purely by academic qualifications.
- Working in partnerships with other disciplines, clinicians and managers, clinicians and the patients/public, others from non-health organisations.
- Involving the public and patients in planning and delivering healthcare.
- Health service management developments: understanding and working with new models of delivery of care; as work-based teams, linking to health action zones, single regeneration bid projects, community development projects and across primary and secondary care interfaces.
- Delivering tangible outcomes: thinking and planning in terms of health gains rather than improvements in structures and systems.
- Research and development: encouraging a culture whereby the two are inextricably linked.
- Health professionals having challenging appraisals.

---

involvement. Professionals are expected to have much broader perspectives of local health needs and to understand the links between health policies, evidence-based clinical care and patient-focused commissioning. Some of the resulting needs are easier to quantify than others.

Learning about health needs assessment is a skill development issue and can be met in a number of traditional and non-traditional ways. It will require health professionals to take a 'macro' view of locality health profiles as well as a 'micro' view about data gathering and public involvement.

Learning in partnership with other organisations may require a different mindset of being willing to share organisational information, develop trust-based relationships and share costs and risks. This will require organisations to behave in non-traditional ways. Such learning cannot be achieved through formal courses or textbooks; it will require action learning, facilitation and the development of learning compacts.[10]

The learning priorities of the NHS are changing as modernisation occurs. Learning is moving towards a strategic function that can provide solutions to issues and can help to manage change in the broadest sense. It should be seen in the context of the healthcare organisation juggling its many priorities and needing to demonstrate tangible outcomes that result in high quality patient care.

Figure 2.2 illustrates the relative overlapping of common priorities for education and training from the primary care organisation's point of view. It illustrates the need for an integrated approach to training and education, as the interdependence of the priorities is clear.

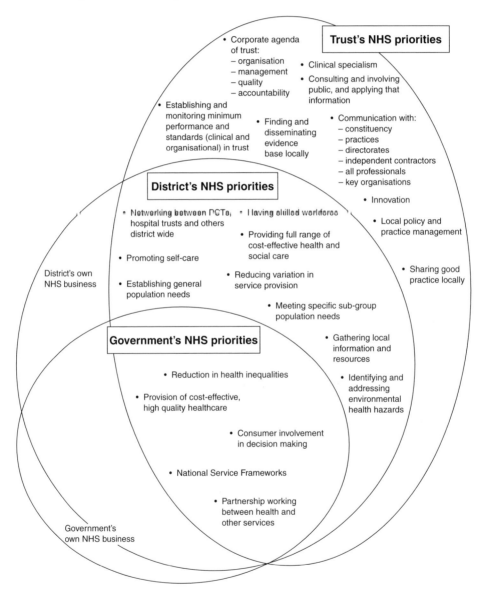

Figure 2.2: Education and training priorities for a primary care trust. Note: The topics given as priority areas for development are examples and are not intended to constitute comprehensive lists.

Figure 2.3 adds the specific elements of overlap from the perspectives of the acute hospital trust, the primary care team and the practitioners. The extent of overlap depends on baseline skills, knowledge and circumstances and the levels of education and training necessary to support the individual's or organisation's roles and responsibilities.

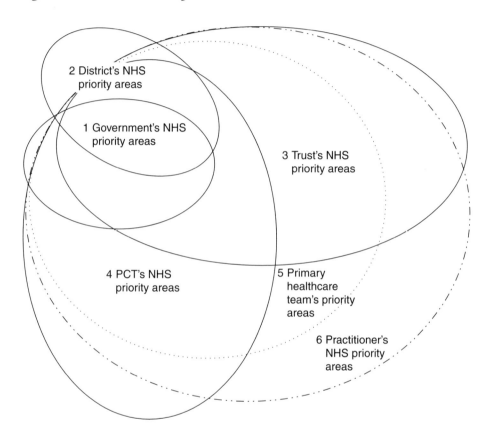

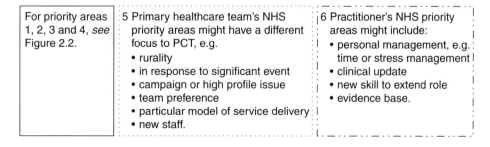

| For priority areas 1, 2, 3 and 4, *see* Figure 2.2. | 5 Primary healthcare team's NHS priority areas might have a different focus to PCT, e.g.
• rurality
• in response to significant event
• campaign or high profile issue
• team preference
• particular model of service delivery
• new staff. | 6 Practitioner's NHS priority areas might include:
• personal management, e.g. time or stress management
• clinical update
• new skill to extend role
• evidence base. |

Figure 2.3: Diagrammatic representation of priority areas of primary healthcare team's and practitioners' perspectives, relative to those of the government, district and trust.

Multidisciplinary education and training

Figures 2.2 and 2.3 both require multidisciplinary education and training for the overlaps in their priorities and common ground. Multidisciplinary education is still quite unusual, although it is a concept that is being developed in healthcare organisations across professional roles and boundaries. Learning together breeds an understanding and develops trust to create a collaborative atmosphere between disciplines, but there is still an underlying commonality of organisation when multidisciplinary learning is conducted in-house. One of the challenges is to break down some of the tribalism and cultural barriers between organisations and learn across a range of organisations, sharing best practice, problems, innovations and producing better patient care as a result.

The practical benefits of multidisciplinary learning are clear:

- cost-effective training and development of core issues with the added benefit of shared experience
- reduced isolation of professional roles (e.g. practice nurses)
- consistency of messages, a common set of values, understanding of mandatory training issues (e.g. manual handling, health and safety, first aid etc.)
- an appreciation of the strengths of diversity of other professionals and the complex nature of professional judgement and ways of working; an understanding of what contributions other professionals can make.

These types of learning arrangements make sense in the changing NHS culture, paving the way for more creative and innovative working arrangements and initiatives at a later date.

There is genuine concern about learning next to a group of professionals who are not familiar with one's own ways of working, and those professional concerns should be taken seriously. There is still a place for uni-professional training but the decision about the mix of professions in the training events should be taken based on the training outcomes expected and not around professional comfort zones.

The Academy of Medical Royal Colleges, Conference of Postgraduate Medical Deans, Council of Heads of Medical Schools, Joint Committee on Postgraduate Training for General Practice, Special Training Authority and Council of Deans of Nursing have published a joint statement about multiprofessional working.[11] They believe that:

- boundaries between professional roles in teams should reflect the needs of the patient, and the competencies of the individuals and their respective responsibilities, rather than the traditional role or rank of professionals
- patient safety must not be compromised by changes in roles

- changes in clinical care should maintain or improve the quality of care for patients
- there should be a positive approach to innovation locally, regardless of its originator
- proposed changes in practice should be carefully reasoned and evidence-based
- changes in roles will require investment in education and training and continuous support from peers, other professionals, employing organisations, regulatory authorities and organisations party to any agreement
- changes in role should be subject to local independent audit and evaluation as part of local governance procedures.[11]

References

1   Department of Health (2000) *The NHS Plan.* Department of Health, London.

2   Department of Health (2001) *Working Together – Learning Together. A framework for lifelong learning for the NHS.* Department of Health, London.

3   Department of Health (2001) *Improving Working Lives for Doctors.* Department of Health, London.

4   NHS Modernisation Agency (2002) *Workforce Matters. A good practice guide to role redesign in primary care.* Department of Health, London.

5   Commission for Health Improvement (2002) *CHI's Combined Annual Report and Accounts 2001–2002.* Commission for Health Improvement, London.

6   Department of Health (2002) *Funding Learning and Development for the Healthcare Workforce. Consultation on the review of NHS education and training funding.* Department of Health, London.

7   National Audit Office (2001) *Educating and Training the Future Health Professional Workforce for England.* National Audit Office, London.

8   Audit Commission (2001) *Hidden Talents – education, training and development for healthcare staff in NHS trusts.* Audit Commission, London.

9   NHS University (2002) *Introducing the NHSU.* NHSU, Department of Health, London.

10   Chambers R and Lucking A (1998) Partners in time? Can PCGs really succeed where others have failed? *Br J Health Care Management.* **4 (10)**: 489–91.

11   Academy of Medical Royal Colleges (2002) *Statement from Academic Medicine and Nursing.* Academy of Medical Royal Colleges, London.

3

Establishing a learning culture

Benefits of a learning culture

Transforming your organisation into a learning organisation will require extensive cultural change. The concept of a learning organisation is not about training alone; it is about developing and utilising the skills, knowledge and abilities of all its employees to ensure optimum performance, while at the same time making life rewarding and fulfilling for individuals.

Taking on learning organisation status is a significant leadership decision, as it will affect everything your organisation does and how it does it – whether it is a general practice, a directorate within a trust, a hospital or primary care trust, a strategic health authority or the Department of Health itself.

It is important that you are clear about the justification for a learning organisation. If it is just the latest management fad or a title to set you aside from similar organisations, it will not work! It is a decision that will require a change or refocus in organisational ethos, strategy, infrastructure, policies and practice. Be clear that your organisation has the stamina and commitment to see through what it starts. It can be damaging to the morale of your workforce to see a new initiative begin with a 'drum roll' and end in a 'hail of bullets'.

What you should be aiming for is a culture that values learning and the ongoing development of staff to ensure that services continue to meet the needs of your patients, any new service developments you want to make and any policy changes. Learning in your organisation should become a process of continual improvement and innovation – an ongoing cycle of action and reflection. It is important that your organisation recognises the true contribution of lifelong learning to the realisation of its goals and objectives. It should underpin your clinical governance processes, change management systems and your implementation programme for national guidance.[1,2,3] This poses several questions which are partly answered in Box 3.1.

- What do you need to establish a learning culture?
- What are the benefits of a learning culture to you as an individual?
- What are the benefits of a learning culture to you as an organisation?

Box 3.1:   Benefits of a learning culture

For an **organisation**, a learning culture can:

- support the development of lifelong learning frameworks within NHS health-care organisations
- motivate staff and improve morale
- improve recruitment and retention record
- reduce the frequency and severity of adverse incidents and risk
- improve organisational performance and effectiveness.

For an **individual**, a learning culture can:

- promote, support and facilitate your continuing professional development
- enable you to use reflection to develop your personal practice and effective-ness
- make you feel valued, empowered and part of a positive organisation
- give opportunities for multidisciplinary, multiprofessional or cross-organisational learning.

All of the items in Box 3.2 are linked and feed into each other. Inevitable underdevelopment in some areas should be acknowledged and addressed over a realistic period of time.

Box 3.2:   Core factors of a learning culture

- Establishing support for creating a learning organisation.
- Shared vision.
- Leadership.
- Empowerment of the workforce.
- Culture that enables learning from mistakes.
- Consumer focused.
- Developing a learning strategy (with associated plans).
- Commitment to teamworking.
- Knowledge management systems.
- Training and development needs analysis.
- Appraisal, performance and personal development plans.
- Identified and protected training budget.
- Opportunity to apply new skills and knowledge.
- 'Getting it right and making it stick.'
- Time for learning and reflection.
- Feedback and evaluation.

Establishing support for creating a learning organisation

You may need to examine your organisation's position and approach to these issues in order to reflect its learning culture development programme as part of the organisational development plan. What you may be beginning to realise is that this is not a job that one person can do in isolation. It will take a group of you with similar views, a range of skills, some common goals and lots of enthusiasm to achieve the changes required in your organisation.

Shared vision

Everyone should know what the purpose of their organisation is at all levels in the organisation. Individuals need a clear sense of direction to ensure that they all work towards common goals and understand what is expected from both them as individuals and their team. This shared vision really represents your organisation's philosophy on lifelong learning and how it intends to develop a learning culture and achieve its objectives. This is the message that your organisation should communicate throughout its workforce that establishes its intent to practise lifelong learning.

Figure 3.1 describes the relationship between the key statements that establish the commitment to develop a learning organisation. The organisational development plan or business plan (the title may vary from healthcare organisation to organisation) is the annual work programme that outlines what it has to do (national and local priorities) and what it needs to do (service and infrastructure developments).

Most organisations will also produce a learning strategy of some description that outlines its policy, standards, infrastructure and working practices for lifelong learning.

Your organisation can communicate its shared vision by using an established mechanism, but the messages should be given using a variety of appropriate methods and media to ensure total coverage of your workforce. Steady and repetitive messages are needed to establish a learning culture.

Leadership

Strong leadership can create and reinforce a learning culture in your organisation, but who are the 'leaders'? In the context of a learning organisation they could be anyone, but they will certainly include the chairman, chief executive, directors, lead clinicians, senior nurses, managers, and education

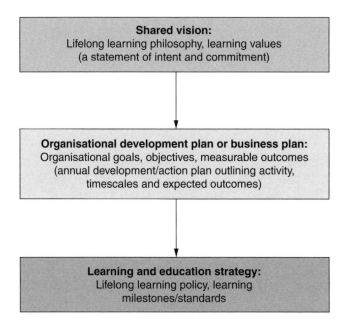

Figure 3.1:   Shared vision and organisational objectives.

and training leads. In fact leaders are those people in your organisation who have responsibility for developing vision, strategic planning, organisational performance, redesign and extension of services, service quality and workforce development.

Learning organisation leaders:

- understand the importance of lifelong learning to achieve service quality
- value everyone's contribution to the organisation's goals and objectives
- value the workforce for their capability and capacity
- invest time and resources in the continual updating of skills and knowledge, understanding that this makes the organisation flexible and able to cope with paced change
- invest in their own continuing professional development and have a current personal learning plan.

Commitment to continued learning from your senior management team should be genuine and visible in a learning organisation – leaders lead by example. This demonstration of a shared vision will ensure that your workforce know what your organisation expects from them and also what they can expect from your organisation in terms of learning support, opportunities and resources for development. Your leaders should also provide a clear statement of the organisation's responsibilities to its workforce on issues of CPD, education and training, and learner support.

This requires explicit action and supporting statements from your leadership and management teams. It is not enough to release policy statements. There should be tangible evidence that key people in your organisation are 'walking the talk', setting an organisational example through their own lifelong learning activity.

One formulation of the leadership role is to direct and co-ordinate the work of others to build, support and work with teams, to work effectively as part of a team and to negotiate and consult effectively. This type of leadership emphasises the 'democratic' concept of team leadership.

Leadership styles vary greatly, ranging from authoritarian to developmental (*see* Box 3.3). The categories are not mutually exclusive, and each style is relevant in the appropriate context.

Box 3.3: Leadership styles[4]

1 **Authoritarian**
Giving clear directions for specific tasks.

2 **Authoritative**
Stating broad objectives and delegating the detailed execution to others while accepting responsibility for the outcome.

3 **Democratic**
Encouraging participation to secure the benefit of the expertise of all team members.

4 **Task orientated**
Focusing on the task in hand and requiring a high standard of task accomplishment, regardless of other considerations.

5 **Developmental**
Focusing on the longer-term development of members of the team as an investment in the future.

Empowerment of the workforce

There needs to be clear, strategic vision and defined organisational values to which the workforce can aspire and contribute and this is the reason for spending some time developing your organisation's shared vision.

There are many practical ways of doing this:

* leadership/management meetings
* policy/special working group
* staff participation and involvement.

There is a fine line between empowerment and anarchy, and traditional organisations may not be ready for an empowered workforce.

Your organisation may have some concerns about 'empowerment', as it is a term which is often misused, seldom understood and rarely defined. Here, we refer to 'empowerment for learning'. This is the pledge by the organisation to develop a learning culture through commitment, proper resourcing, fair access to learning support and ensuring that the learning infrastructure is in place. Empowerment for learning also requires a commitment from the workforce. Their contribution is to accept responsibility for their continuing development, reflective practice and participation in lifelong learning. This form of empowerment is really a learning contract between your organisation and its workforce based on both parties' commitment to develop skills and knowledge, shared responsibility and effective healthcare delivery.

There should be opportunities for two-way communication. Staff involvement through representation at the policy formation stage is desirable and your organisation should have a mechanism in place already to achieve this. Communication between the management and staff should not be a token gesture but should have real value in the organisation and may be effected through your organisation's team briefing process, or primary care trust open meetings with staff, for example.

Individual members of staff in your organisation also need to have ownership over the ways in which they work and learn. Personal development planning can provide this when conducted in a positive and meaningful way. The individuals should be able to identify their learning needs and have access to basic tools that enable them to identify their learning style preferences so that they can identify the most effective training/development activities for them.

It is recognised that individuals learn best when:

* they take responsibility for their own learning
* they are involved in the planning, content and evaluation of learning
* they use past experiences in the learning process
* individual needs and styles are recognised
* learning is relevant to the context in which they work.[5]

Culture that enables learning from mistakes

Developing a blame-free culture is not the sort of ideal that many traditionalists would believe possible in the NHS. Strong reporting systems that highlight adverse events and 'near misses' but do not disadvantage or stigmatise the reportee are of paramount importance. It can be a difficult balance to achieve – encouraging people to report but not tolerate poor performance. Your organisation will probably already have such a mechanism in place but people may not be clear how to use it. It may be worthwhile reviewing it in the light of developing a learning culture.

The learning process should be open and encourage everyone to feel responsible for maintaining high standards of patient care and organisational functioning. Learning from errors and near misses requires insight and, once that has been gained, some evidence of changed behaviour and practice should automatically follow. The key is to ensure that the learning from such systems has a direct route into your organisation's corporate planning process. Failure to do this could result in repetition of the same errors.

Where insight is not present, rigid processes for robust risk management and critical incident analysis systems are essential. Issues related to learning from adverse events and for developing learning cultures are explored in detail in national guidance.[2,6]

Consumer focused

Healthcare users and carers are traditionally underused as a learning and education resource. As the purpose of your organisation is to serve the needs of patients you should be actively engaging patients and the public in the planning and delivery of new service developments and the education of clinicians and healthcare workers. This is not an exact science and methods are improving all the time. Learning organisations should begin the process and learn from experience. *See* Chapter 8 for more material on the meaningful involvement of patients and the public in improving the quality of patient care and services.

Despite clear direction from the Department of Health, public/patient involvement in the design of service delivery has, with certain exceptions, been more 'lip service' than a reality thus far. Service development and training programmes have been designed to reflect what are perceived as patient needs: better communication, service delivery as close to home as possible and limited waiting times. However, in reality, it has generally been healthcare professionals and professional managers who decide what patients want, rather than patients or the general public themselves.

There are reasons to believe that patients may have different perspectives to those of professionals. Attempts at developing patient senates and *professional* patients have largely floundered. It is not clear what role a *professional* patient would fulfil. Once a process of professionalisation has occurred, the utility of that person's input is degraded. What the health service needs is informed patient input into the design of services throughout the organisation.

Developing a learning strategy

The learning strategy outlines the standards and framework for learning and from that should come the implementation plans that deliver the outcomes, e.g. organisational development plan, business plan, clinical governance action plan etc.

Commitment to teamworking

Teamworking promotes and facilitates informal learning by developing an appreciation and understanding of the roles and skills of others. It also encourages sharing and support and improves communication skills to ensure increased knowledge. Your organisation's objectives are probably (largely) achieved through teams, and therefore good teamworking is vital. Team delivery of healthcare strengthens the need for team learning. Your organisation should ensure that there is a framework in place that encourages and supports team learning. It will probably be multidisciplinary which is even better, as multidisciplinary training and shared learning helps to promote corporacy, empowerment and understanding.

Your team is more likely to function well if it:

- has clear team goals and objectives
- has clear lines of accountability and authority
- has diverse skills and personalities
- has specific individual roles for members
- shares tasks
- regularly communicates within the team – formally and informally
- has full participation by team members
- confronts conflict
- monitors team objectives
- gives feedback to individuals
- gives feedback on team performance
- has external recognition of the team
- has two-way external communication between the team and outside world
- offers rewards for the team.[7]

A team leader with a democratic style enables a team to function well and encourages rather than imposes change.

Knowledge management systems

Efficient information systems are vital to knowledge management and performance monitoring. Extensive development of electronic information systems and associated training programmes for all staff will ensure up-to-date information is accessible and used appropriately to inform service development. They will also facilitate data collection for audit, which may be used to measure and compare performance and identify areas where change is required.

Your organisation will have developed an information strategy in line with national guidance, *Information for Health*.[5] It will outline the infrastructure and may even include education and training requirements, but it is important in a learning organisation to understand the significant role of information as communication too. A clear picture of what information processes (electronic, paper-based and verbal) exist and how they are maintained and accessed is an essential element of knowledge management in a learning organisation.

Explicit information is easy to capture but how could your organisation capture the learning outcomes of networking, crossing professional and organisational boundaries to develop knowledge and expertise, or the use of mentors or preceptors for newly qualified staff?

Training and development needs analysis

In order to ensure that everyone has the skills needed to carry out their individual roles, an assessment should be carried out of people's training and development needs. This should anticipate any needs relating to probable service changes. The way in which assessment is undertaken in your organisation may be clearly defined but the ultimate focus should be around the needs of *patients*. A well-designed needs analysis will ensure that the most appropriate training and development approach is provided for each individual and in a way that recognises each individual's preferred learning style. Your organisation could integrate the needs analysis process into the organisation's appraisal or personal development planning cycle, if it has not already done so.

Your needs analysis process may involve interviews, surveys or performance data, or the identification of core competencies might be used to assess development needs for each professional and service group. Clinical care pathways define the way in which a service is delivered around a patient and could therefore be used to identify development needs of healthcare and support workers and promote teamwork. It is useful to review your existing systems in the light of an emergent learning culture.

Appraisal, performance and personal development plans

Appraisal is another demonstration of the commitment of your organisation to learning and should take place at least on an annual basis by an appropriate person. Appraisal is a formative and developmental process, which is being introduced for general practitioners and hospital doctors working in the NHS, across the UK and in other disciplines. While the details of the appraisal system will vary for various specialties and disciplines the educational principles remain the same. The aims of the appraisal system are to give members of staff regular feedback on their previous and continuing performance and to identify and plan to meet their education and development needs.

An appraisal provides a mechanism for identifying development and training needs from both the individual's and the organisation's perspectives. There should be a balance between your organisation's requirements and individuals' aspirations for learning. There should also be an effective feedback system from individuals' appraisals in order to identify and anticipate skill gaps across the organisation. This is a key part of a learning organisation and helps to set the culture.

Personal development plans should be based on identified learning needs and individuals' aspirations and should be in place for all members of staff. Personal development plans will help to ensure that applications to attend training events and undertake learning activities are valid and appropriate. They will also enable your organisation to develop relevant and timely opportunities for development across teams and disciplines.

Educational appraisal has been a well-known concept for a number of years. In educational appraisal, the individual learner reviews his/her educational status and plans future developments. The appraiser facilitates this process. Educational appraisal has important features such as confidentiality and is seen as being entirely separate from assessment. In appraisal for medical consultants working within the NHS, evidence of adequate performance is brought to the appraisal and is subsequently used in the process of the doctor's revalidation of his/her professional qualifications, as well as considering his/her educational needs. Consultant appraisal in the NHS should have three outputs:

- an educational plan
- evidence of standards of practice and learning for revalidation
- evidence of their competence demonstrated to the medical director.

The need for appraisers who understand the principles of appraisal and an initially hostile consultant body have made significant demands on hospital trusts to provide training in both being an appraiser and being appraised. The need for ongoing training in these skills will continue. Doctors working in general practice are in a similar situation.

Identified and protected training budget

The identification and protection of a training budget is key, as funding streams are not always clear and explicit. Your organisation should clarify the access to, and quantity of, funding that is available and communicate its commitment to lifelong learning in a tangible way.

Funding streams have been streamlined but there are still strong divisions between funds that are labelled for uni-professional use. The identification of a training budget requires the organisation to map the training funds that are available for all professions and staff groups to gain a clear idea of the total resources available. If your funding streams are fragmented throughout your organisation, it may be a useful and enlightening experience to quantify a unified budget and do some basic analysis including proportion of organisational budget, resource per head, main areas of spend, gaps and duplication etc.

Box 3.4 proposes what a trust's learning and development budget should pay for.[8]

Box 3.4: What a trust's learning and development budget should pay for[8]

NHS learning and development funds must support:

- higher education tuition costs for all students not yet in salaried employment studying for healthcare professional qualifications other than for courses funded through the Higher Education Funding Council for England
- bursary costs for degree and diploma students undertaking healthcare courses in higher and further education.

The NHS learning and development funds should contribute consistently and significantly to:

- educational innovation and developments linked to the NHS Plan, service modernisation and the NHS lifelong learning agenda
- the costs to NHS organisations of practice placements.

In partnership with the individual and his/her employing organisation, the learning and development funds must support:

- tuition costs for people working in NHS organisations undertaking continuing personal and professional development
- the costs of developing staff without a recognised professional qualification through further and higher education within the skills escalator approach
- salary costs of doctors and dentists undertaking postgraduate training
- salary costs of NHS employees undertaking continuing personal and professional development.

Consideration should also be given to funding the following:

- support for capital costs of the educational infrastructure within NHS organisations, in partnership with the organisation concerned
- supporting capital developments in higher education, underpinning healthcare education and development.

Opportunity to apply new skills and knowledge

Individual learning can help to shape organisational development when opportunities are provided for staff to apply new skills and knowledge. New-found skills are very quickly lost if they are not practised.

What mechanisms does your organisation have in place for the systematic application of new skills and knowledge and is the impact of those measured in terms of individual, team or organisational performance?

'Getting it right and making it stick'

Making improvements in organisational effectiveness is essential in the current NHS climate but there is a danger that change is made for change's sake. It is straightforward for organisations to identify pockets of good practice but the key to creating a learning culture is providing real evidence that there is consistency in application and sustainable improvements. This may require the leaders in your organisation to give positive reinforcement where good practice is found and establish a systematic way of cascading success throughout the organisation, at all levels. Reflect on the processes that exist in all levels of your organisation that could facilitate this positive reinforcement and cascading of knowledge. This will ensure that your organisation gets it right, and opportunities for frequent application and practice will 'make it stick'.

Time for learning and reflection

In order to take advantage of opportunities for development it is vital that learning time is provided. Time is needed both to learn and also to reflect on learning, to ensure that knowledge and practice do not stagnate. Team learning will be dependent on having sufficient and protected time and adequate resources.

Many organisations are formulating policies that recognise both individual and team learning opportunities and are defining standards for 'protected' learning time and resources. It is important to note that the arrangements need to be made in the context of the organisation's equal opportunities policy for staff so as to ensure that this is not breached. The way in which time for education and training is organised, protected where necessary and backfilled in your policy should be explicit.

The principle of equal opportunity should apply to employment, training, education, and the provision of goods, facilities or services. The principle of equal treatment guarantees members of your workforce freedom from discrimination on the grounds of sex, pregnancy, marital status, family status and sexual orientation.[9]

Box 3.5:   Everyone has to work at creating equal opportunities for disabled colleagues

A pilot study of primary care workers reported that colleagues often did little to enable disabled doctors and others to work in general practices.[10] For example, changes had not been made to the workplace or systems in general practices to help to retain disabled doctors and staff at work. It appears that those who develop physical disabilities or chronic ill-health while working in the NHS may not disclose details about their impairments to others and that it is common for colleagues to ignore their additional needs.

Feedback and evaluation

People like to know that they are doing a good job and also want to know when they have made a mistake. Such feedback is too important to leave until an annual review and should be given on a regular basis. Reflective practice is an ideal way to evaluate the impact of the learning on the learner. It is a valuable part of developing professional practice and personal effectiveness, and can be carried out by the learner on a weekly or monthly basis.

Your organisation's training and development activities should be evaluated properly by the learner to ensure that his/her needs have been met and that any inappropriate or inadequate training does not continue, from the organisation's point of view. A robust evaluation system needs to be in place to ensure that the outdated 'happy sheets' that ask individuals to score the venue, tutor and refreshments do not constitute the evaluation of learning. It is much better if evaluation is focused on learning outcomes and the extent of the application of learning in practice.

Kirkpatrick described four levels of evaluation in which the complexity of the behavioural change increases as the evaluation strategies employed ascend to higher levels.[11] Figure 3.2 illustrates the Kirkpatrick hierarchy. Evaluation of reaction will include satisfaction or happiness; evaluation of learning will cover the knowledge and/or skills acquired. Evaluation of behaviour will include the transfer of learning to the workplace; evaluation of results will cover the transfer or impact of the activity on society.

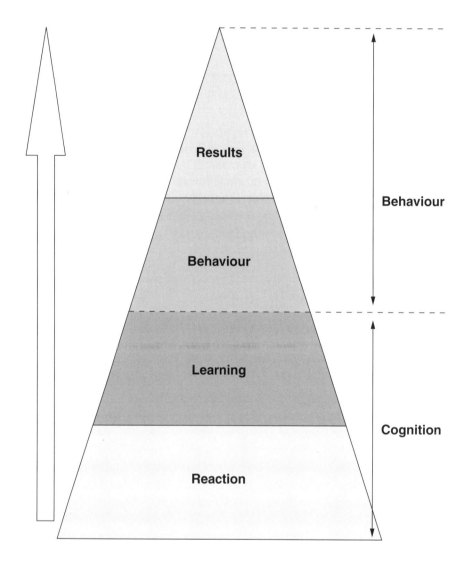

Figure 3.2:   Kirkpatrick's hierarchy of levels of evaluation.[11]

Competencies in healthcare

Most professions have their own set of core competencies, which are published
and provide a framework for capability and professional practice.

There is no single, accepted way of drawing up a list of competencies.
Methods used involve observation and interviewing or the use of existing lists
with local modification following interviews or questionnaires.

Whether to adopt competencies as indicators for quality improvement or
performance management is an organisational decision, which may be influenced by the undertaking of a quality award such as Investors in People.

Box 3.6: Competence

Competence requires knowledge, appropriate attitudes and observable mechanical or intellectual skills which together account for the ability to deliver a specified professional service.[12]

There are a number of common themes that are reflected in the definitions of competence. These are:

- knowledge, understanding and judgement
- a range of skills – cognitive, technical or psychomotor, and interpersonal
- a range of personal attributes.[13]

Occupational standards describe what people need to be able to do in employment in 'ideal' terms. National occupational standards describe what should happen and what should be achieved, and are structured to include:

- *performance criteria* – how you know that the outcome is the right quality
- *range* – situations and contexts to which the standard applies
- *knowledge specification* – what the individual needs to know, understand and apply to achieve the outcome
- *evidence requirements* – types and sources of evidence required to prove that the outcome has been achieved.[14]

'Competencies' are the knowledge, skills, abilities and behaviours that an employee applies in performing his/her work and are the key employee-related levers for achieving results that are relevant to the organisation's business strategies. A 'competency framework' is a set of competencies and includes associated behaviours that link directly to overall strategic priorities and the work that needs to be done to achieve them, as well as to levels of proficiency for each behaviour. The framework provides the proficiency levels and behaviours required for a specific job or jobs.

Box 3.7: Example of implementation plan to develop competency frameworks[14]

The initiative was delivered over a number of phases that were evaluated and amended at each stage.

- Phase 1 – pre-development meeting.
- Phase 2 – prepared an implementation plan for the project.
- Phase 3 – trust requested participation of nurses in the interview stage.
- Phase 4 – individual interviews held.
- Phase 5 – analysed results and prepared draft competency frameworks.
- Phase 6 – focus groups refined draft competency frameworks.
- Phase 7 – presentation of the competency frameworks and proposed implementation plan.

The proficiency ladder implemented in the trust described in Box 3.7 was adapted from Benner's 'novice to expert' model in which she identified five levels of proficiency:

1   novice
2   advanced beginner
3   competent
4   proficient
5   expert.[15]

Benner used this model to define levels of practice in nursing. She defined the levels as follows:

- **Novice:** that stage in skill acquisition where no background understanding of the situation exists, so that context-free rules and attributes are required for safe entry and performance in the situation.
- **Advanced beginner:** one who can demonstrate marginally acceptable performance. The advanced beginner has enough background experience to recognise aspects of a situation.
- **Competent:** a stage in skill acquisition typified by considerable conscious, deliberate planning. The competent stage is evidenced by an increased level of efficiency.
- **Proficient:** the proficient performer perceives situations as wholes rather than in terms of aspects, and performance is guided by maxims. The proficient performer has an intuitive grasp of the situation based upon a deep background understanding.
- **Expert:** developed only when the clinician tests and refines theoretical and practical knowledge in actual clinical situations – so an expert has a deep background understanding of clinical situations based upon many past cases.

A similar approach was used in the case study described in Box 3.8.

Box 3.8:   Competency profiling in health informatics – a case study

The NHS Information Authority (NHSIA) produced a health informatics competency profile (HICP) relating to the informatics skills necessary for the implementation of the *Information for Health* strategy document.[5] This was then used in a survey designed to cover the full range of professional staff groups in the NHS and all of the topics contained in *Information for Health*. Competency levels to assess the skill and knowledge levels in health informatics for each staff group are defined below.

continued opposite

HICP skill levels

Code	Level	Definition
0	None	No skills or knowledge are required in this topic
1	Basic	A basic awareness and few, if any, skills
2	Intermediate	Moderate skills and knowledge
3	Advanced	Specialist skills and knowledge
4	Expert	Full skills and knowledge

The full reports, both profile and survey, are available (at the time of writing) online from the NHSIA's website at http://www.nhsia.nhs.uk.

And finally ...

Although learning is undertaken by individuals, organisational arrangements can foster or inhibit the process of learning. The organisational culture within which individuals work in healthcare settings shapes their engagement with the learning process. Lifelong learning by the NHS workforce is one significant way of improving healthcare.[16]

References

1 Department of Health (2001) *Shifting the Balance of Power.* Department of Health, London.

2 Department of Health (2000) *An Organisation with a Memory.* Department of Health, London.

3 Department of Health (2000) *Improving Working Lives.* Department of Health, London.

4 Rashid A and McAvoy P (2002) Managing to be a successful leader. *GP.* **30 September**: 40–2.

5 Department of Health (1998) *Information for Health.* HMSO, London.

6 Department of Health (2001) *Building a Safer NHS for Patients.* Department of Health, London.

7 Hart E and Fletcher J (1999) Learning how to change: a selective analysis of literature and experience of how teams learn and organisations change. *Journal of Interprofessional Care.* **13 (1)**: 53–63.

8 Department of Health (2002) *Funding Learning and Development for the Healthcare Workforce. Consultation on the review of NHS education and training funding.* Department of Health, London.

9   Equal Opportunities Commission (1998) *Equality in the 21st Century.* Equal Opportunities Commission, Manchester.

10   Moloney R, Hayward R and Chambers R (2000) A pilot study of primary care workers with a disability. *Br J Gen Pract.* **50**: 984–5.

11   Kirkpatrick DJ (1967) Evaluation of training. In: R Craig and J Bittel (eds) *Training and Development Handbook.* McGraw-Hill, New York.

12   World Health Organization (1988) *Learning to Work Together for Health. Report of a WHO study group on multi-professional education for health personnel: a team approach.* WHO, Switzerland.

13   International Council of Nurses (2001) *International Competencies for the Generalist Nurse.* ICN, Geneva.

14   Storey L, Howard J and Gillies A (2003) *Competency in Healthcare – a practical guide to competency frameworks.* Radcliffe Medical Press, Oxford.

15   Benner P (1984) *From Novice to Expert: excellence and power in clinical nursing practice.* Addison Wesley, California.

16   Davies HT and Nutley S (2000) Developing learning organisations in the NHS. *BMJ.* **320**: 998–1001.

4

Targeting the learning organisation at improving the quality of health service delivery

Unlike in industry where *profit* is the bottom line, the *service* we deliver to patients and relatives in healthcare is the bottom line. If turning a service delivery unit into a learning organisation does not improve service delivery then not only is your effort a waste of time, but it is also a waste of resources that could have been utilised elsewhere. No-one could doubt that some training is necessary; you could not ask a school-leaver to surgically remove a pituitary gland or counsel a grieving mother. The argument in favour of a learning organisation goes beyond that and states that, in the medium-term, service provision will be enhanced by making learning an integral and central part of day-to-day activities in a healthcare workplace.

All learning may have some intrinsic value, but having a consultant neurosurgeon go on a course to learn Sanskrit will be of less direct value to the organisation than involving the surgeon in a programme of education directed at improving communication skills.

National Service Frameworks

During the last two decades of under-investment in the NHS, organisations have delivered services within their available resources and patient demand, but this had local anomalies built in. There was little standardisation across the *National* Health Service of the UK and this resulted in 'postcode access' for patients for certain aspects of healthcare.

As learning organisations, healthcare providers need to generate confidence in their services from staff, patient and public perspectives in order to develop modern healthcare services.

The government has identified a number of priority areas for the NHS. Some may argue about the priorities that have been chosen, but improvement has to start somewhere. Identifying areas of particular deficiency is a good strategy and as a democratically elected government the people's representatives have a right to direct the NHS to the areas that they consider important. As part of the overall strategy a number of National Service Frameworks have been developed for England (*see* Box 4.1).

Box 4.1:   National Service Frameworks and Plans (England) with publication dates

Mental health	1999
Coronary heart disease	2000
National cancer plan	2001
Older people	2001
Diabetes	2001–2002
Renal services	2003
Children's services	2003
Long-term conditions (neurology)	2003

National Service Frameworks (NSFs) provide sets of national standards that promote consistency and evidence-based care. An NSF has, for the first time, provided a published, national standard and core of information about disease management and treatment pathways across all levels of the NHS in England. Primary and secondary care providers have milestones against which to measure their progress in providing standardised care.

The frameworks are produced by gathering the best scientific evidence, looking at how that evidence should influence practice and then setting out a series of targets for the implementation of that practice within the NHS (as in Box 4.2). The main underpinning strategies are: information management and technology; research and development; resources (revenue and capital including the built environment and equipment); workforce planning; and planning and performance.

Box 4.2:   Structure of National Service Frameworks (NSFs)

NSFs vary in their structure, but elements of the following are present:

- aims
- standards
- rationales
- effective interventions
- service models
- audit and evaluation
- immediate priorities
- milestones for service delivery
- performance indicators – holding the NHS to account.

The standards in the frameworks are useful for planning education and training as they can underpin the curriculum or content of a training programme.

Standards tend to be the broad overarching concepts that are achieved through specific interventions and delivered through service models. A standard sets out the quality of care or services which should be delivered.

Service models determine how services should be delivered and can also be wide-ranging. Service models describe how services should be delivered. They can be wide-ranging but also quite specific. The more explicit these are, the more likely they are to be effective. Examples could include setting up or organising specific services in a particular way.

Interventions are broadly about what needs to be provided.

The milestones determine how quickly the standards will be implemented. Milestones may take some time to implement and will depend on the resources becoming available. The milestones should therefore spell out the steps along the way to delivering the standard with dates specified; they should be specific and measurable.

Performance indicators should be meaningful and feasible (i.e. collectable). Performance indicators include the setting of indicators to measure progress towards the successful implementation of the overall strategy.

By providing targets within the NSFs the government is providing interim and end points against which performance can be judged. This performance can be assessed by a variety of methods, from crude statistics, as in waits before admission, through to the more in-depth techniques such as those used by the Commission for Healthcare Audit and Inspection (CHAI). The challenges provided by the NSFs have and will result in organisations having to configure themselves to meet those targets and this will have implications for staff training. For example, the NSF for Older People expects each acute hospital trust to have a functioning stroke unit, or at least to have stroke patients cared for by experts in that field, by 2004. This will require the identification and training of a cohort of staff to fulfil the requirements of the NSF.

There is a general need for healthcare organisations to reconfigure themselves to be more patient-friendly. Not only is this part of government policy, but asking patients about their experience of the care they have received is also a central plank of the CHAI assessments.

Clinical governance

A lot has been written about clinical governance – what it is and how to do it. What you should focus on is the learning process linked to clinical governance and how a learning culture can embed clinical governance as habitual practice.[1,2]

Clinical governance requires all individuals and teams involved in the delivery of healthcare services to examine what they do, set against a clear picture of service requirements, and then measure their effectiveness and any skill or knowledge gaps they have. This requires healthcare professionals and managers to measure and analyse current practice, define and adopt service standards, measure results and make necessary changes. In fact, to demonstrate basic audit and re-audit cycles, learning can take place at any stage as is normal practice for many clinicians engaged in meaningful continuing professional development.

Clinical governance in a learning organisation is a whole-system, quality improvement process that depends on the interactions of a wide variety of people – clinicians, managers and support workers and, in some cases, professionals from other organisations. The complexity of modern care pathways means that, in some situations, individuals from primary and secondary care organisations need to learn together to improve the interfaces of health and social care and improve the overall service that the patient receives.

By using clinical governance as a vehicle for determining service quality it is possible to use established criteria to examine specific aspects of service quality from service users' or service providers' perspectives. Effectiveness, acceptability, efficiency, access, equity and relevance are key criteria for measuring service quality[3,4] and provide valuable, shared learning opportunities.

This approach opens clinical governance up as a multiprofessional, multidisciplinary learning opportunity. You should not be confined by the traditional view of measurement but develop new quality indicators that meet the requirements of you as the provider and your service users.

The UK government has brought in a system of clinical governance partly in response to the events that occurred in Bristol (*see* Box 4.3) with regard to clinicians' problems in assessing their own performance. This is also as part of a broader movement towards accountability. Clinical governance is an evolving concept. It initially started out as a concept of safe individuals working within safe systems in safe organisations. It now encompasses much more. The chief executive of an acute hospital trust or primary care or mental health trust has statutory responsibility for clinical governance within that trust. It is no longer solely the individual clinician's responsibility that patients get the correct treatment but a shared responsibility between the organisation and the individual.

Box 4.3:   The Bristol Inquiry noted that:[5]
- there was no requirement for hospital consultants to keep their skills and knowledge up to date or to demonstrate to anyone other than their peer group that they remained sufficiently skilled
- the systems in existence were not capable of assuring the competence of healthcare professionals
- poor or diminishing competence could not be adequately addressed until it became manifestly bad.

The advent of appraisal for the medical profession is central to the development of clinical governance. For many years nursing staff have had personal development planning, but appraisal for medical staff is something new and not altogether welcomed by the profession.

Quality improvement

The concept of a learning organisation is one of regeneration and quality improvement while understanding the importance of the individual's contribution to the quality of care provided by a healthcare organisation, working to the best of his/her ability. The obvious link for healthcare organisations to make is between clinical governance and a learning culture. Prior to the introduction of clinical governance in the NHS, service quality was considered in a piecemeal fashion. It was the remit of each organisation to have quality systems in place, but what those covered and how they were monitored were not subject to a national framework of standards.

Some organisations simply used the standard medical model of managing clinical risk, while others used some of the management models based on Total Quality Management (TQM)[6] and the popular quality text *In Search of Excellence.*[7] Clinical governance standardised the quality improvement approach by providing a nationally recognised standards framework for quality improvement, risk management, audit and evidence-based care.

Table 4.1 illustrates Deming's 14 points[6] which are crucial to quality improvement. Deming's points are interpreted in the context of developing quality through a learning organisation infrastructure in the right-hand column of the table. The focus is to engender quality in service provision by valuing individuals' and teams' contributions and by directly linking the taking of responsibility for learning to do things better to service improvement and increased patient satisfaction.

Organisations should be explicit in these messages and expectations. It is not realistic to assume that all healthcare workers feel a pride in what they do without any direction or guidance. Organisations now have the clinical governance framework for that direction but it is not enough on its own. It needs a process for ownership throughout the organisation, with continuous learning and development to support it.

Health inequalities

There are gross health inequalities within the UK. On average a male person from the lower socioeconomic groups in society lives 3.5 years less than someone from the higher socioeconomic groups. Racial minorities also have

Table 4.1   Quality improvement in a learning organisation: Deming's 14 points[6]

Deming's 14 points	Learning organisation perspective
1 Create constancy of purpose	1 Learning philosophy and vision of quality
2 Adopt the new philosophy	2 Adopt philosophy statement of intent
3 Cease dependence on inspection	3 Infrastructure for reflective learning
4 Cease awarding business on price alone	4 Evaluation of learning outcomes and use results to redefine value for money
5 Improve continuously and forever	5 Integrate learning culture into clinical governance, risk management and corporate planning activities
6 Institute training and retraining on the job	6 Systematic education and training strategy led by workforce's identified needs, e.g. skills escalator
7 Adopt and institute leadership	7 Develop leadership, learning champions and change agents
8 Drive out fear	8 Create culture enabling people to learn from mistakes
9 Breakdown barriers between staff	9 Multidisciplinary shared learning
10 Eliminate slogans and targets from the workforce	10 /11 Change focus from counting to health outcomes
11 Eliminate numerical quotas and goals	
12 Remove barriers that rob people of pride in workmanship	12 Promote learning as investment in workforce; empower them to take responsibility for their learning
13 Institute a vigorous programme of education and self-improvement	13 Lifelong learning policy
14 Put everyone in the organisation to work on the transformation	14 Communicate philosophy, visions and infrastructure to all

shorter life expectancy. How much the health service can compensate for the consequences of socioeconomic deprivation and ill-advised behavioural patterns is a moot point. However, at least the NHS should not be party to the continued disadvantage of minority groups and the socioeconomically disadvantaged.

One method of ensuring that an organisation serves a population well is for the workforce to be representative of, and drawn from, that population. If there is a significant ethnic minority group population locally then a healthcare organisation should ensure that it recruits a reasonable number of workers from that community. More challengingly, you should ensure that people from the minority group are represented at all levels within the organisation.

Health Delivery Plans lie at the heart of the modernisation programme and represent a wide based health strategy for improving the health and well-being of the population. They require the collaboration of service providers to offer more up-to-date, user-focused services that meet identified health needs and achieve health gains.

Partnership development and multiagency working

In a learning organisation the word 'partnership' carries significant implications for commitment, sharing, openness and valuing diversity. Opportunities to work and learn with others add a new dimension to any organisation. It can broaden perspectives, add capacity and capability to the workforce and can produce results that would not be possible if the partners worked separately.

There are different types of partnerships and Figure 4.1 illustrates the partnership typology allowing organisations and teams to identify their partnerships and understand the context in which they operate.[8]

Consultant/advisor partnerships are usually based on experts being used for their specialist knowledge. The outcomes of the partnership between the NHS and external consultancies may involve developing new processes and skills or developing new tasks, but the learning is from one partner's expert knowledge. Business partnerships are based on developing new initiatives and consist of partners pooling their expertise and applying the knowledge to a project. Both of these types of partnership tend to be restrictive in nature, governed by clear boundaries, rules and regulations.

Collaborative partnerships are usually concerned with developing new structures and configurations in changing environments. The learning comes from the partners sharing their experiences and perspectives to produce answers to emergent problems. Strategic alliances are innovative learning partnerships that operate in uncharted territory. They learn together, sharing risks, resources, contributions and benefits, and discovering and applying new knowledge. For strategic alliances to work well, power and information should be shared, as in Box 4.4.

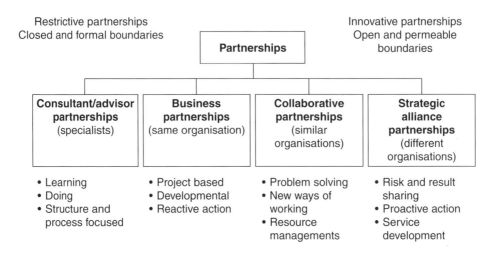

Figure 4.1:   Partnership typology.

Box 4.4:   Example of a successful strategic alliance

A strategic alliance was created within a primary care group (PCG) in England. Allied health professionals, social workers, carers, service users and voluntary organisations participated in a focus group to begin to identify the needs of their local population and report back to the PCG's board. They used a skilled facilitator to achieve their objectives and to capture the joint learning that took place. They evaluated the impact that the focus group had made six months after the event and they also examined how they had learned together. They identified what worked well and what they could do to make future events even more effective. The results were then shared throughout the participating organisations in the form of an evaluation report, and similar events could then use the recommendations as a checklist.[9]

Both collaborative and strategic alliance types of partnerships are classified as 'innovative' and are open – sharing information, vision and goals. They are not governed by a rulebook but are based on understanding and respect, valuing each other's diversity. Those involved in partnership or multiagency working can use this typology to understand the learning substructure of such relationships. This will enable the partnerships to utilise the available learning mechanisms to capture new knowledge, skills, behaviours and attitudes for the benefit of the wider organisation(s).

Partnerships that produce effective results have a set of critical success criteria embedded in their structure as seen in Box 4.5.

Box 4.5: Critical success factors of learning partnerships

- Shared vision and ratified partnership agreement.
- Commitment to achieving common goals.
- Clear understanding of each other's roles and responsibilities.
- Joint strategy and implementation plan.
- Partners value the diversity of the partnership and respect each other's contributions.
- Clear decision-making processes.
- Partners have parity and equal access to information.
- Commitment to sharing resources.
- Equal sharing of risks and benefits.
- Flexibility to accommodate partners.

Reflective practice

Reflective practice, in a quality improvement context, is about looking back to analyse situations, events and actions critically, deconstructing them to understand their component parts, the influencing and causal factors, and identifying why the resulting course of action was chosen. This process enables individuals, teams and organisations to understand problem-solving, decision-making and information flows at a 'micro' level, which in turn allows the identification of ethical, empirical and partnership learning, resulting in effective practice (*see* pages 4–5).

In learning organisations reflective practice becomes a state of mind. A learning culture constantly encourages and enables individual practitioners to 'notice' what they do in their day-to-day work and to identify areas of improvement. The mechanisms that trigger this automatic response are the learning mechanisms instituted by the organisation. In the context of quality improvement it would include clinical governance activities, such as audit, clinical supervision, significant event analysis, adverse event recording systems and personal/professional development planning.

There is no 'right way' to practise reflection. It is a thinking process which may involve verbal or written articulation. It should result in action that helps the practitioner to understand or resolve a situation or issue. The overall aim of reflective practice is self-improvement and the development of professional practice whether the practitioner is a clinician, a manager or a support worker. The individual in a learning organisation is responsible for his/her commitment to reflective practice but the learning organisation needs to place a high value on the outcomes of the process and create the right environmental conditions to support it.

The organisation needs to provide protected time and space to allow reflection to happen habitually. This is a difficult condition to create in healthcare organisations that may not have a full complement of staff to deal with an extremely hectic work programme. Some professional groups may be more badly affected than others, e.g. many hospitals have high numbers of nursing vacancies, which they have difficulty filling.

What the learning organisation has to achieve through cultural change is to remove the guilt that people feel about 'thinking about themselves and their own work' and to give a higher value to the products of reflection – identifiable and improved service quality. The learning environment should support reflective practitioners by creating a safe environment to learn from mistakes,[10] where the outcome is learning in a better way – not retribution and punishment. When reflective practice is viewed in this way the great importance placed on the organisation's learning philosophy and infrastructure is clear. Continuous improvement in service quality and patient safety should follow if reflective practice is supported by the organisation's leaders and implemented systematically.

Risk management in a learning organisation

It would be virtually impossible for any organisation to achieve best-value-for-money services while thousands of pounds were being lost each year in putting mistakes right. Errors are costly and unacceptable. Litigation costs can be estimated, but how can the cost of damage to patients, damaged reputations, loss of patient trust and public confidence in the service be evaluated?

The NHS is a highly complex organisation delivering sophisticated treatments. At times health professionals are working right on the frontiers of medical knowledge so that some errors are inevitable. The dilemma is how to minimise the risk of error without compromising the existence of innovation and medical advances.

A continuous improvement process is required to identify risks, analyse significant events, strengthen systems and improve practice, to prevent as many errors as possible occurring in the first place. Those in the organisation can choose the most suitable process for them but should give considerable thought to what they need the process to do for them and how it fits into their learning culture. In Table 4.2 the most common quality initiatives are explained in terms of structure and expected outcomes, along with some useful notes.

Table 4.2 Quality initiatives compared

Quality initiative	Structure	Expected outcomes	Notes

Investors in People (IIP) award	National quality standards to improve businesses' effectiveness through their people.
	    Costs vary from region to region and are based on requirements. Approx £1500 for small organisations. Assisted funding from the government may be available.
		National recognition and award. Detailed benchmark of current position and plan for moving forward.
		    Overhaul of training and development strategy.
		    Robust system for workforce development.
			To gain full benefit IIP should be conducted as an organisational cultural initiative and not just as a process exercise.

Quality Charter Mark	Nationally recognised award for public service organisations based on performance of customer service. Assessment on ten criteria (pre-2003) and six criteria (post-2003). Costs: £750 plus VAT.	National recognition and award. Detailed audit and assessment process. Work can be tailored to meet NHS priorities e.g. user involvement, clinical governance etc.	Assessment tools used are really useful to understand a service from the user's perspective. Particularly useful for partnership development.

BS 5750 (British Standard) ISO 9001 (International Standard)	Quality management system for British/ international industry. Focus on manufacturing processes, quality systems and procedures. Costs: significant variance; approx £3500 for assessment but needs annual review.	National recognition.
		    Some suppliers require this standard.
		    Building of robust systems and quality assurance measures.
			The assessment process can be cumbersome and last 6 to 12 months.

EFQM Excellence Model® (sometimes referred to as the Business Excellence model)	Commercial quality framework offered to public sector organisations by accredited consultants. Limited recognition. Costs: dependent on consultancy used.	Effective framework that provides a whole organisational development approach. Needs total commitment from organisation's leadership. May require significant change to organisation's structure.	Very powerful framework if the whole organisation is 100% committed.

continued overleaf

Table 4.2   *continued*

Quality initiative	Structure	Expected outcomes	Notes
Total Quality Management	Commercially available tool for quality improvement, which can be implemented by a trained/knowledgeable internal facilitator. Costs: variable, but includes cost of initial training, internal restructuring, meetings etc.	Robust framework for benchmarking, audit, quality team development, evaluation and action. Process can be integrated into the organisation.	Effective and home-grown option but totally dependent on the quality of the facilitator and his/her skills.
Royal College of General Practitioners Quality Awards[11]	Range of quality initiatives geared specifically for general practice/primary care including: • Fellowship by Assessment (FBA) • Membership by Assessment of Performance (MAP) • Quality Practice • Quality Team Development (QTD) • Accredited Professional Development (APD). Costs vary depending on scheme, e.g. approx cost £3000 per organisation (QTD).	Quality assessment and improvement frameworks tailored specifically to general practice and primary healthcare teams.	Quality awards are offered for individual GPs and practice teams.

Quality improvement methodologies

Whichever models or quality initiatives your organisation chooses it is important to remember that they will not explain why:

- people produce better results if they feel that their contribution and ideas are valued and taken seriously
- service users value the quality of communication and personal care as highly as the surgical intervention or treatment they receive

- self-monitored quality systems are more effective than inspected quality systems.

The quality models simply advocate the behaviours and processes that engender these things as good practice for everyday application.

The rationality of the medical model (scientific, quantitative methodologies) may produce scientifically sound results but it cannot always provide answers for the diverse NHS patient base. Quality improvement needs both to be truly effective – the rational, quantitative medical model and the qualitative, intuitive models of patient involvement.

Integration of national, local and organisational priorities in a learning organisation

An integrated approach to quality improvement through learning is one of the clearest benefits of a learning organisation. The ability to plan the delivery of national, local and organisational priorities strategically by maximising the capacity and capability of the workforce is deliverable through a learning culture.

Organisational leaders require insight to promote the bigger picture to their workforce, providing them with a clear context and an objective-led work programme. The professional groups within the healthcare organisation can take responsibility for developing their practice in line with organisational priorities, their professional code of practice and their continuing professional development, effectively reinforcing their professional ethics and identity.

Organisations should strike a balance between professional standards, organisational responsibility and personal responsibility, for service excellence and patient safety. Many organisations are unfamiliar with the blurring of professional roles and responsibilities that multiagency working creates, and professional groups may struggle against a perceived loss of professional identity. Opportunities to reinforce the value of multiagency working and the achievement of common goals should help this co-operative process.

These mechanisms improve critical analysis and reflection skills, clarifying quality improvement processes. Quality standards generated by learning organisations need no enforcement. These processes continually reinforce a culture of quality through shared learning and best practice.

References

1   Chambers R and Boath E (2001) *Clinical Effectiveness and Clinical Governance Made Easy* (2e). Radcliffe Medical Press, Oxford.

2   Chambers R and Wakley G (2000) *Making Clinical Governance Work for You.* Radcliffe Medical Press, Oxford.

3   Donabedian A (1992) Quality assurance in healthcare; the consumers' role. *Quality in Health Care.* **1**: 247–51.

4   Maxwell RJ (1992) Dimensions of quality revisited: from thought to action. *Quality in Health Care.* **1**: 171–7.

5   Bristol Inquiry report is available on the web at http://www.bristol-inquiry.org.uk/final_report.

6   Deming WE (1986) *Out of the Crisis.* Cambridge University Press, Cambridge.

7   Peters TJ and Waterman RH (1989) *In Search of Excellence.* HarperCollins, New York.

8   Garcarz W and McGraw J (1999) *Partnership Development Between Higher Education and Birmingham Health Authority.* Birmingham Health Authority, Birmingham.

9   Northfield Primary Care Group, Birmingham, July 2000.

10 Department of Health (2001) *Building a Safer NHS for Patients.* Department of Health, London.

11 Quality Unit, Royal College of General Practitioners, 14 Princes Gate, Hyde Park, London SW7 1PU – for details.

5

Practical tools to build a learning organisation

This chapter contains a series of exercises and tools that can help your organisation to start its journey towards becoming a learning organisation, whatever its current size or setting. It is not an exhaustive toolkit but does cover key activities that your organisation may need to complete that will support you in the early stages of development.

The tools and exercises follow a logical sequence and each has a quick reference guide and outline of when to use the exercise, how long it will take and what resources you need (if any) to complete the exercise successfully. The guidance will help you to implement each tool with the right expertise and at the right level and to allocate enough time.

Exercises 1 to 9 focus predominantly on the planning and implementation of a lifelong learning philosophy and culture. Exercises 10 to 16 focus on the design and structure of learning events, including the identification of training needs and the evaluation of the effectiveness of training activities. Exercise 17 specifically addresses research and learning partnerships.

In order for this section of the book to be helpful to all we have included some very basic tools as well as those requiring more expertise. The frameworks, toolkits and proposed generic training programmes included here are representative of the types of developmental support available. Your organisation may have developed its own tools or exercises. The idea is to select what you find useful and adopt approaches that reflect the nature and needs of your organisation.

Quick reference guide to what resources are involved
🕐 = Time
☺ = Whether facilitation is needed

Level of difficulty
① = Simple and straightforward
② = Needs expertise and/or specialist knowledge and skills
③ = Challenging

Exercise 1: Establishing the *raison d'être* for your learning organisation

This exercise will help your organisation to justify the decision to move towards being a learning organisation. The exercise can be used as either a strategic organisational development task with the senior management team, a management objectives task with the operational management team, or a staff involvement exercise with the whole workforce or staff representatives. The best results are produced when the exercise is conducted with small groups where people can discuss and debate the implications.

Quick reference guide to Exercise 1

🕐 = 60 to 120 minutes

☺ = External facilitation helpful for objectivity

③ = Challenging, important to retain focus

In your groups spend time reading the statement below that describes a learning organisation and reflect on what this may mean for your organisation. Discuss and answer the questions (Box 5.1), making a final recommendation from your group about whether your organisation should become a learning organisation.

A learning organisation continually renews and develops its capability and capacity for change by:

- promoting a philosophy and culture that ensures lifelong learning opportunities for the whole workforce with an outcome of improved patient care
- ensuring that its workforce is competent and confident to complete their duties
- valuing people's experience and contributions to quality improvement through involvement in corporate planning and reflective practice, improving service delivery
- sharing a clear picture of what the organisation's goals and priorities are with the whole workforce
- actively including patients and service users in learning activities to improve responsiveness and create effective, patient focused services
- providing all staff with an opportunity to reflect on their practice, review their performance, identify their training needs and develop their skills and knowledge
- systematically evaluating organisational performance in all areas relevant to learning and improvement.

The resulting benefits include improved staff morale, increased retention of skilled staff, being more responsive to changing goalposts, proactive planning, better control and crisis management, improved financial and operational management and an enthusiastic and innovative workforce.

Box 5.1:   Your discussion questions

1   How does this differ from our current approach?

2   What will a learning organisation deliver that we do not have at the moment from the following perspectives:
    (a) organisational
    (b) management
    (c) team
    (d) individual?

3   What current barriers exist that could disrupt the creation of a learning organisation?

4   How could we combat these barriers?

continued overleaf

5   What opportunities would a learning culture give us as an organisation?

Conclusion: As a result of our discussions the group recommends that:

Exercise 2: Creating a strategy and statement of intent

The development of any type of strategy requires commitment and action from the organisation's leadership, to give it authority and agency. A learning strategy is about developing an environment that nurtures learning and a culture where learning is integral to individuals' roles and the organisation's business processes. Just to share knowledge throughout an organisation is not enough; it is about the sustainable change and improvement that results from shared knowledge.

This exercise (*see* Table 5.1) is intended to offer a framework for senior managers and key stakeholders to identify which of the success criteria they already have, or are working towards, in the development of a learning organisation strategy and statement of intent. The exercise can be incorporated into a standard planning meeting or can be used as a structure for a dedicated working/policy group, focused on the creation of a learning culture or organisation. The discussion to establish your current status will vary from 30 minutes, if the exercise is used as a simple checklist, to up to three hours, if it is used as part of a developmental event.

Quick reference guide to Exercise 2

🕐 = 30 minutes to three hours
☺ = In-house facilitation
① = Simple and straightforward (if used as checklist)
② = Needs expertise and/or specialist knowledge and skills (part of development event)

Table 5.1　Checklist for what makes a strategy and statement of intent

Criteria	Where are we now?	Your action
1　Strategy and statement of intent are specifically constructed with lifelong learning values at the centre.		
2　Specific standards relating to access, funding, resources, protected time. Minimum requirements are drawn up and apply to all employees who want to undertake training/education.		

continued overleaf

Table 5.1   *continued*

	Criteria	Where are we now?	Your action
3	Representatives of the workforce are involved in the development of policies and implementation plans.		
4	The strategy, statement of intent and implementation plan are communicated throughout the organisation using the appropriate mechanism, e.g. team briefings.		
5	Evaluation methods are developed to measure effectiveness, outcomes and contribution to organisational objectives.		

Exercise 3: Planning the learning organisation development programme

The checklist below (*see* Table 5.2) offers a sequence of events for the development of a learning organisation. The plan is based on a basic Gantt chart which you can adapt to your own timescales. It is particularly effective as a project plan with senior and operational managers.

Quick reference guide to Exercise 3
🕐 = 90 minutes to set up, minimal monitoring time
☺ = No facilitation needed
① = Simple and straightforward

Table 5.2   Plan your timetable for the activities and tasks of your intended programme

Activities and tasks	*Timescale (days, weeks or months)*
Develop justification and vision for learning organisation	
Create strategy and statement of intent	
Complete timetable for developing a learning organisation	
Implement a communication plan for staff involvement, team briefing etc.	
Development of relevant policies, lifelong learning, education and training, protected learning time etc.	
Integration of planning and learning	
Corporate planning cycle begins: establish organisational goals and priorities (e.g. SWOT exercise – *see* pages 70–71)	
Implementation plan: infrastructure and resource matrix	

continued overleaf

Table 5.2   *continued*

Activities and tasks	Timescale (days, weeks or months)
Develop education and training plan: skills escalator, core programmes, shared programme etc.	
Integration of learning and key functions: clinical governance, risk management, complaints, public and patient involvement	
Develop evaluation process	
Develop research and development programme	
Regular review process to check progress and capture learning	

Exercise 4: Policy checklist and key indicators for lifelong learning strategy

The following checklist should be completed early on in the process of forming a learning organisation. It highlights a range of policies common to learning organisations and a brief overview of their contents. Most organisations will have their own version of most of these policies but they may need to be reviewed to ensure that they reflect lifelong learning values. This exercise can be conducted within operational management groups or with a broader audience of staff representatives or staff involvement groups.

The exercise can be used to take a snapshot of the organisation's status of integrating lifelong learning at a policy level. This simple use of the checklist takes a look at each policy and helps those using it to assess policy content and identify key lifelong learning indicators.

The checklist (*see* Table 5.3) could also be used with a specific policy development group, lifelong learning focus group or a learning organisation implementation group to construct policies and develop strategies. The simple application could take as little as 30 minutes to complete, while the more detailed specific application could take up to three hours, depending on the nature of the group and what the objectives of the session are.

Quick reference guide to Exercise 4
🕐 = 30 minutes to three hours (dependent on detail)
☺ = In-house facilitation
① = Simple and straightforward

Table 5.3 Determining policy and content of a learning organisation

Type of policy	Overview of contents
Lifelong learning	Values and standards for lifelong learning, organisational commitment, statement of intent, management role, infrastructure that supports lifelong learning, responsibilities of the workforce.
Education and training	Framework for access, funding, skills escalator, standards and minimum requirements. Rules for internal and external programmes, induction programme, training needs analysis process, application process.
Continuing professional development (CPD)	CPD framework, portfolio requirements, professions' requirements and documentation samples.
Study leave	Rules and requirements, access and process, application forms.

continued overleaf

Table 5.3   *continued*

Type of policy	*Overview of contents*
Mentoring/coaching/ secondment	Partnership arrangements, scheme framework, training implications, learning contract, mentoring/coaching agreement, confidentiality, application process.
Performance appraisal	Appraisal framework, process, training needs analysis, objective setting guidance, training requirements, frequency, line management responsibility.
Risk management	Framework, standards, processes, tools, reflective practice, reporting system, feedback loop.
Clinical governance	Process, mechanisms (audit etc.), standards, responsibilities, feedback loop.
Quality improvement	Process, mechanisms (significant event analyses etc.) standards and responsibilities, feedback loops.

Note: the policies listed in Table 5.3 may interrelate with each other and it is important that the areas of overlap are highlighted. Policies establish the corporate governance of the organisation and it is important that policies are regularly reviewed to ensure that they reflect the changes in the environment. The policies also lay out the organisation's infrastructure and provide evidence that the organisation has mechanisms in place to deliver support to those responsible for providing and delivering the service.

Table 5.4 encourages the identification of evidence and good practice within learning organisations. It offers generic examples that illustrate learning cultures at work and allows parallel examples of real practice to be drawn. This exercise would be used by the same target groups as those using the policy checklist (*see* Table 5.3), but at a later stage to measure progress in the process of developing a learning organisation. Some organisations may wish to use the exercise to shape their policy or strategy on learning organisations.

Table 5.4   Evidence of key indicators of organisational learning

Key indicator	*Organisational examples*
Empirical learning Learning that takes place throughout the lifespan of employees, policies and systems in a planned and intentional manner.	
Ethical learning Evidence of organisational commitment for professional and personal learning; learning that is part of the quality improvement cycle; patient participation programmes; and learning through complaints procedures and risk management systems.	

continued opposite

Table 5.4   *continued*

Key indicator	*Organisational examples*
Partnership learning Evidence of cross-boundary learning with other organisations, professions, social care and voluntary sector organisations, curriculum development with further education and higher education institutions and external training providers.	

Exercise 5: The basic planning process

The planning process must start with an assessment of where the organisation is currently, what influences it and what factors affect it – as in Figure 5.1. Consider the environment – the immediate conditions and factors that influence the organisation.

Environmental perspectives include:

- political
- economical
- sociological
- technological factors.

Political economical sociological technological (PEST) analysis

A PEST analysis (*see* Box 5.2) is a simple tool that focuses on factors external to the organisation, allowing analysis of drivers that may or may not be within the organisation's control.

Undertaking a PEST analysis, as part of Exercise 5, should be carried out in the context of the broader picture – the climate in which the organisation operates. The context needs to reflect the perspectives and issues of other healthcare providers, patient groups and the target population and the current local political situation. It should draw on relevant profiles, audits and surveys.

Strengths weaknesses opportunities threats (SWOT) analysis

A SWOT analysis (*see* Box 5.3) is a simple tool that allows you to analyse the internal factors that create the current situation within an organisation. Undertaking a SWOT analysis, as part of Exercise 5, focuses on the internal factors that drive the organisation forward and give it purpose. The SWOT analysis will reflect the vision of the organisation, its strategies, objectives and priorities, its functions and its 'rules' of how it engages with others. Information that would be helpful to underpin the SWOT analysis includes the range of services provided and financial information, costs, cash flow etc.

The planning process shown in Figure 5.1 is adaptable for executive teams defining their organisation's future purpose. Alternatively, a directorate or general practice team who wish to plan their organisational objectives could use this as a template for a team-building event over a half or whole day.

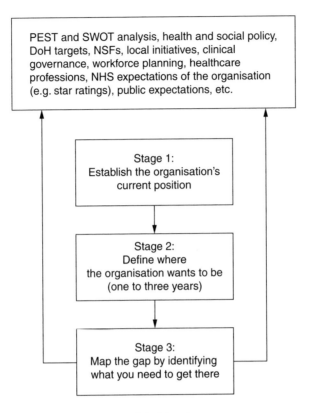

Figure 5.1:   The simple three-stage model of the planning process.

Individuals who want to plan their personal development could also use a similar process and spend a couple of hours formulating their personal development plans.

Quick reference guide to Exercise 5
🕐 = Two hours to a whole day (dependent on application and target group)
☺ = Little or none required for individual use; external facilitation may be useful if used as a whole-day session
① = Simple and straightforward when applied to a small group
or
② = Challenging if used as a whole-day event

Box 5.2:   PEST analysis

Discuss the political, economical, sociological and technological factors that influence your organisation's aims and objectives.

Political	Economical
Sociological	**Technological**

Box 5.3: SWOT analysis

Identify the internal control factors (strengths and weaknesses) and the external control factors (opportunities and threats) that influence you or your organisation's ability to achieve its aims and objectives.

Strengths	Weaknesses
Opportunities	**Threats**

Exercise 6: Infrastructure and resource matrix

This exercise will help you to assess the readiness of your organisation's infrastructure in the development of a learning organisation. The following key in Table 5.5 explains the symbols used in the matrix to help you to plot gaps in resource availability.

Table 5.5 Key for Exercise 6

Symbol	Infrastructure/resource	Explanation
	Documentation	Policy, protocols, standards, operating procedures etc.
	Location	Physical location, available space, training facilities etc.
	Money	Protected/identified funding, budgets, bids, grants etc.
	Expertise	Skills, knowledge, capability, competence within or without the organisation, training and education provision.
	People	Appropriately trained and available staff, staff hours, coverage for training etc.
	Materials	Equipment, books, training resources, supplies, provisions etc.
	Information technology	Hardware, software, networks, internet capability, library facilities, knowledge management systems.
	Communication	Communication flows, mechanisms, e.g. newsletter, team briefing, user involvement, community, media and press.
	Planning	Planning mechanisms, planning groups, project management capability, strategic planning meetings, links to DoH and front-line staff.

Table 5.6 can help you to plot your organisation's resources by ticking where there are identified resources available and making a cross where there are none. By identifying these gaps you can begin to build an action plan of the next steps in your journey towards becoming a learning organisation. This exercise can be used by teams, directorates or the organisation as a whole to identify resource needs.

Quick reference guide to Exercise 6
🕐 = One to two hours (depending on group and detail required)
☺ = In-house facilitation
① = Simple and straightforward

Table 5.6 Plan the resources you will need for your intended learning organisation (please note that all columns should be appropriate for each aspect of your organisational infrastructure)

Infrastructure	Resources								
Equal opportunities policy									
Education policy									
Education/training budget									
Training needs analysis process									
Induction programme									
Core training programmes: mandatory, specialist									
Library facilities									
Teaching facilities									
CPD policy									
Personal development plans									
Appraisal/performance reviews									
Study leave/protected learning time initiatives									
Policy for clinical placements or supervision									
Quality assurance for external education/training providers									
Systematic evaluation for education/training									

continued overleaf

Table 5.6   *continued*

	Resources								
Infrastructure									
Clinical governance monitoring									
Risk management processes									
Partnership learning with other organisations									
Curriculum development with HE and FE institutions									

Exercise 7: Developing a training and education strategy

Developing a training and education strategy is a key requirement for a learning organisation as it outlines major investment in skills and knowledge and shapes the organisation's capability and future capacity. The flowchart in Figure 5.2 gives a logical, stepped process to follow.

Developing the strategy can be tackled in a variety of ways. Senior managers may be tasked with drawing up a draft strategy, or it may be the responsibility of a single manager or directorate – or it may be that a specially convened multiprofessional group may be required to lead the development.

The task may be broken down into stages and a range of people involved with developing specific aspects of the strategy. Alternatively, the various stages may be incorporated into existing planning processes, such as at a priorities planning meeting, or when setting management objectives etc.

Quick reference guide to Exercise 7

🕐 = 30 minutes to whole day (depending on staged approach)

☺ = Some experienced facilitation required

③ = Challenging; need to maintain focus and utilise knowledge and experience

---

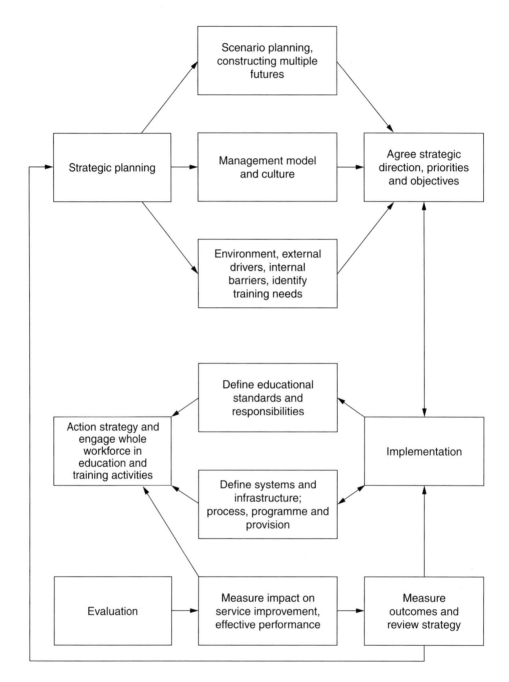

Figure 5.2:   Flowchart for developing an education strategy.

Exercise 8: Developing an education and training pathway in a learning organisation

Education and training pathways are the arteries for any learning organisation as they carry its life-force of people working in development and performance. Pathways define the parameters of the learning and define its 'home' in terms of where the responsibility for the programme's delivery and evaluation sits. Two worked examples of how to use these tools are given below (*see* Boxes 5.4 and 5.5).

Quick reference guide to Exercise 8 (relevant to Box 5.4)
◷ = One hour (basic pathway planned)
☺ = No facilitation required
① = Simple and straightforward

Box 5.4: Education and training pathway development

Learning/training need identified: Providing a skills escalator for all non-professional support workers wishing to gain formalised qualifications within healthcare.

Target group(s): Domestic or support staff, administration and clerical staff

Uni-professional	☐	Multidisciplinary	☐	Partnership learning	☐
Specialist	☐	Generic	☐	Team learning	☐

Levels of training:
Introductory ☐ Basic ☐ Intermediate ☐ Advanced ☐

Method of accreditation: National Vocational Qualifications and NHS learning accounts.

Validation required: Induction programmes, basic skills training modules, NVQ programmes.

Pathway routes: Human resources/training department: clerical, medical secretaries, receptionists, nursing, healthcare assistants programme.

Outline content of various components: Basic literacy and numeracy modules, European Computer Driving Licence (ECDL), appraisal and personal development planning, entrance to NVQ of choice.

Delivery methods: Varied, work-based modules, taught sessions, computer-based modules etc.

Related training programmes: Further education basic skills modules, health and safety, manual handling, cross-infection modules etc.

Potential providers: Local colleges, primary care trust, local acute trust training department etc.

Learning programme outline (Box 5.5)

This planning sheet can help you to plan specific, formal learning programmes that meet identified needs within your learning organisation. Educationalists, trainers and line managers can use it to map out programme outlines as a first step to developing formal training modules. Vocational training is relatively straightforward but the development of more formal, academic programmes usually needs to follow the institution's own format. This tool can still be used as a starting point for joint development in learning partnerships.

Quick reference guide to Exercise 8 (relevant to Box 5.5)

🕐 = One to two hours (dependent on complexity of the module/programme)
☺ = No facilitation required
② = May need some expertise or specialist knowledge to develop fully a training programme or module

---

Box 5.5:   Learning programme outline, e.g. developing clinical team leaders

Programme leader/provider: Clinical governance lead and external training provider.

Pathway: CPD doctors/nurses. **Qualification/accreditation:** CATS points from local university.

Programme duration: 30 taught hours and 30 hours' self-directed study over six months.

Target group: General practice clinical teams. **Levels:** Postgraduate/professional.

Programme rationale
- To develop clinical team leaders within general practice teams to take over-all responsibility for clinical governance, risk assessment and significant event analysis processes within the team.
- Maintain up-to-date knowledge and skills that promote clinical effectiveness throughout the team.
- Develop skills that support changing clinical practice across the team, motivation, performance monitoring, identification of training needs and CPD planning.

Prerequisites
- Clinician/nurse currently employed in a general practice team with minimum of one year's experience.
- Active interest in clinical effectiveness, personal and professional development.
- Experience of practical research and/or evidence-based practice.

continued opposite

Learning objectives and expected outcomes
- To develop clinical team leaders that lead on clinical effectiveness within the practice team.
- To improve clinical effectiveness and service delivery for practice population.
- To implement risk management procedures that contribute to clinical effectiveness.
- To implement systems that promote evidence-based practice and clinical audit.

Outline content
- Self-assessment skills audit (benchmarking).
- Clinical governance – the context, defining the issues.
- Presentations and setting up a group session.
- Defining clear objectives.
- Motivating people through change.
- Quality improvement models.
- Measuring performance.
- Self-assessment skills audit (needs assessment).

Key theories/evidence base used
- Evidence-based practice/clinical audit/clinical governance/setting clinical standards.
- Design, delivery and evaluation of training session/identification of training needs.
- Motivation/change management/appraisal/giving and receiving feedback.

Learning assessment methods
- Project work/coursework/observation/coaching against university criteria.

Training resources required
- Course materials/library facilities.

Evaluation methods
- Module assessment, presentation, observation, 2500 word assignment.

Related programmes: Teaching certificate, supervisor management certificate.

Exercise 9: Induction flowchart

Induction is a fundamental building block for developing learning organisations. It establishes a culture of learning for every new member of staff. It enables the consistent establishment of corporate standards, behaviours and responsibilities. The following chart given in Figure 5.3 establishes key stages and functions of induction in a healthcare organisation. Operational managers and those with specific responsibility for education and training should input into the development of an effective induction programme.

Quick reference guide to Exercise 9

🕐 = One to two hours (depending on complexity of the programme)

☺ = No facilitation required

② = May need some expertise or specialist knowledge to fully develop a training programme/module

---

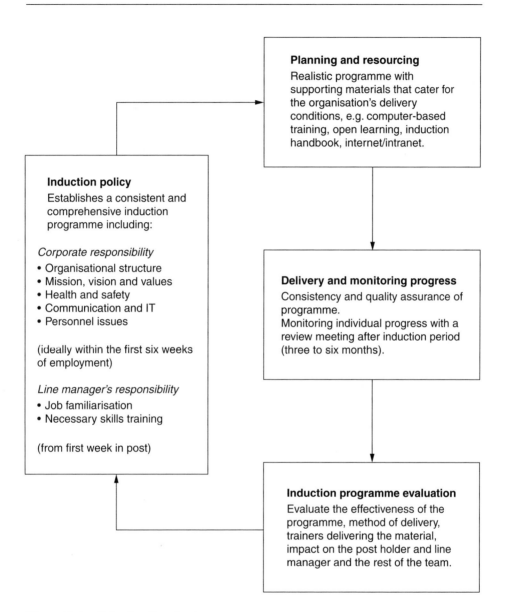

Figure 5.3: Induction flowchart.

Exercise 10: Learning methods in learning organisations

Table 5.7 outlines the methods commonly employed in learning organisations, the learning styles catered for and their strengths and weaknesses. It can be used by anyone designing or delivering training programmes to assist them in making learning experiences productive for all delegates or trainees.

The learning styles typology used is the Honey and Mumford model.[1] Details and questionnaires are available from www.peterhoney.com.

Quick reference guide to Exercise 10

🕐 = 15 minutes to two hours (depending on quick reference or structured programme design)

☺ = No facilitation required

② = May need some expertise or specialist knowledge to apply to a whole training programme/module

---

Table 5.7 Strengths and weaknesses of various learning methods and their relation to people's preferred learning styles

Learning method by preferred learning style	Strengths	Weaknesses
Reflective practice including: learning journals, significant event analysis and clinical supervision. Reflectors, pragmatists.	Routed in existing practice; transferability of learning very good. Not costly to run.	Requires insight to be effective. Some may need support to develop reflective skills.
Secondments including: job share, shadowing and secondment (inside and outside of the organisation). Activists, reflectors.	Creates empathy and a better understanding of others' difficulties and priorities. Encourages valuing diversity.	Needs a simple framework to ensure learning expectations and outcomes are identified and disseminated.
Mentoring: internal and external mentoring. Reflectors, pragmatists.	Very effective for professional development of specialists/professionals.	Dependent on the skill, approach and commitment of the mentor. Needs an agreement to formalise the arrangement.
Coaching/supervision: learning buddy schemes, tutorial support for distance learning, career, executive and skills coaching and formal debriefing. Pragmatists, reflectors.	Encourages learning partnerships, empowerment and initiative. Offers a safe environment to explore sensitive issues.	Outcome dependent on the quality of the coach/supervisor. Needs an agreement that ensures confidentiality and defines parameters of the arrangement.

continued opposite

Table 5.7 *continued*

Learning method by preferred learning style	Strengths	Weaknesses
Action Learning Sets (ALS) including journal clubs, developmental or problem solving, facilitated and self-managed. Activists, pragmatists, reflectors.	Developmental, creative and innovative method. Very cost-effective; captures and identifies organisational talent.	Can lose focus and effectiveness over a long period. Requires committed and enthusiastic people to make them successful.

Quality circles: self-directed and specifically funded quality improvement groups.
    Activists, theorists, pragmatists, reflectors.
 	
Open access learning: resource centre (actual or virtual) that gives access to learning resources and training packages 24 hours a day, seven days a week.
    Activists, theorists, reflectors.
	Small groups (six to ten) with specialist knowledge gather around the problem and produce creative solutions. Quality improvement of high value and sustainable as it has a high level of ownership. Use of technology gives greater flexibility for the learner.	Need to be properly funded to run tests/pilot solutions. Needs commitment from senior and line managers to empower group to make change and see it through. May be costly to set up; needs a co-ordinator to manage the facility.

Distance learning packages: computer- or paper-based materials for self-guided learning. Theorists, reflectors.	Huge variety available. Suits reflective and theoretical learning styles. Flexible for learners to fit into their timetable.	Can be expensive to purchase or develop in-house. May need additional tutorial/learner support.
Vocational training programmes: National Vocational Qualifications, generic skill programmes, first aid etc. Activists, pragmatists.	Nationally recognised qualifications to generic standards.	Programme structure may not fit in with organisation's methods and learning styles.
Academic programmes: university certificate, diploma, degrees. Theorists, reflectors (pragmatists depending on the curriculum).	Offers a high standard of professional and personal development; motivating and brings latest theories and practices into the organisation.	May not be cost-effective solution for the organisation. Difficult to tailor to specific development needs. Transfer of learning may be problematic.
In-house training programmes. All styles can be catered for in the design of the programmes.	Can be tailored specifically to the organisation's or target groups' needs.	Quality dependent on the trainer delivering the material. Resource-hungry, location, resources, time to co-ordinate.

Exercise 11: Constructing and conducting user surveys

There is a much greater emphasis on staff and patient or public (user) involvement in a learning organisation nowadays, as they are seen as a key resource for the development of learning programmes. Some simple tips can help your organisation to get the most from its staff and user involvement schemes.

The checklist in Table 5.8 should be helpful to anyone working with the public, patients and users.

Quick reference guide to Exercise 11
🕐 = One to two hours (dependent on complexity of the event/questionnaire)
☺ = Using checklist requires no facilitation
② = May need some expertise or specialist knowledge to fully develop an event
     or questionnaire

Table 5.8   The dos and don'ts of staff and patient involvement exercises

When developing a staff or patient involvement survey: dos	When developing a staff or patient involvement survey: don'ts
Try to include people who are a fair representation of the target group.	Don't involve the same people over and over again – change your groupings.
Use questionnaires and interview surveys to gather information and views.	Don't conduct surveys/questionnaires without explaining to users what you are doing and who will see the information.
Think of creative ways to include the views of people who do not ordinarily take part in surveys, for whatever reason.	Don't assume that because no-one has complained, the service you offer is perfect – ask for opinions.
Begin with an easy group and include some experienced representatives; they ensure some quality data to analyse.	Don't discuss personal cases (remember confidentiality); instead, keep to an agenda and talk in general terms.
Use a structure and procedures to ensure that your results are valid. Learn how to sample your target groups, how to conduct questionnaires ethically and gain informed consent.[2]	Don't use leading or ambiguous questions with patients or staff. Be clear about the information you require and record responses accurately.
Choose the right method for the task you want to complete.	Don't assume that there is the skill/ knowledge of research within your team to undertake surveys. If it is there, identify and use it; if it is not, develop it.
Use the exercise as a two-way communication process by ensuring feedback about the results is shared with those who contributed.	Don't ask for information you will not use – people will require feedback about the positive ways that you have used their comments to improve service provision.

Exercise 12: Significant event audit or analysis

This process analyses real situations (good and bad) to enable teams or individuals to understand what happened, why it happened, who were the key people involved and how an adverse significant event can be prevented in the future or a successful event can be repeated on a regular basis.

Significant event audit or analysis can encompass all aspects of service delivery – operational, managerial and clinical – and should be viewed as a constructive process that offers significant learning for the whole organisation.

It is a very cost-effective and accessible method of quality improvement as it relies on members of the team and/or organisation meeting together to discuss and learn from the event. The method contributes to good risk management and can be enjoyable and motivating when the event analysed is an example of good practice or success.

The process covers four basic stages:

- select the event you want to analyse
- gather the data needed
- hold a meeting to analyse the event and agree on action
- implement action and review the effects.

The following checklist in Table 5.9 can be used in the review meeting to ensure that all aspects of the event are covered. It can be used by an individual, in a team meeting or by a whole directorate to assist them in analysing significant events, identifying good practice, highlighting potential and actual risks and working up solutions to deal with them.

Quick reference guide to Exercise 12

🕐 = One to two hours (dependent on the nature of the significant event)

☺ = No facilitation required

② = May need some specialist knowledge to fully analyse the event and identify the risks

---

Table 5.9   Significant event audit /analysis checklist

	Detail	Result
Event to be analysed		

Issues	*Action*	*Results*
How was the event managed initially?		
Who was involved?		
What were the positive things that occurred?		
Could anyone else have contributed to the event?		
How could they have contributed?		
What were the key factors that determined the outcome?		
Were there any interface issues?		
Were there any team issues?		

continued opposite

Table 5.9 *continued*

	Detail	*Result*
Event to be analysed		

Issues	*Action*	*Results*
Follow-up arrangements: • How and when will change be implemented?		
• What action/policy decision will you take as a result of this audit/analysis?		
• Who will be responsible for ensuring that this is done?		
• When will the task be completed?		

Exercise 13: Continuing professional development checklist

This simple checklist (*see* Table 5.10) can provide individuals or teams with a clear purpose and picture of the range of CPD tools and activities.

Quick reference guide to Exercise 13

🕐 = 15 minutes (used as quick checklist)

☺ = No facilitation required

① = Simple and straightforward

Table 5.10   Purpose of various tools used for continuing professional development

Tool and process	Purpose
Personal development plan (PDP)	To review recent performance (one year), to define where the individual wants to be in one year's time and to highlight any development needs that need to be met in order to get there. Needs to reflect organisation's objectives and professional's development aspirations. All healthcare professionals, clinicians, nurses, managers and support workers should have an annual personal development plan.
Significant event audit or analysis	A regular process that allows the individual to evaluate professional practice and the resulting outcomes critically with a view to identifying good practice or learning and service needs, and evaluating improvements. Clinicians may feel that clinical events need to be dealt with separately but the process can be used for all significant events, involving organisational and clinical components.
CPD portfolio	A file that reflects aspirations, objectives, educational, training and development needs, underpinning evidence that those needs have been/are being met and a record of learning and professional development. Some professions have issued members with a specific format or folder, but it is the process that provides the greatest value.
Professional practice (or workplace) development plans	To review the practice's or workplace's performance as a whole (e.g. at one year) to define where the clinicians and management team want the practice or unit to be in a year's time, to define what resources the practice/unit needs to get them there (e.g. money, people, training and equipment) and what tasks need to be done in order to get them there.

The flowchart in Figure 5.4 shows the relationship between types of CPD activity and the process of personal development planning. CPD pathways are unique to the individual but the learning organisation has a responsibility to support their creation through its policies of open access, supported development, well-resourced opportunities and protected planning and learning time. Individuals thinking about their CPD, and managers planning CPD programmes for teams or directorates, can use this model to ensure a cohesive approach that reflects personal and professional development requirements.

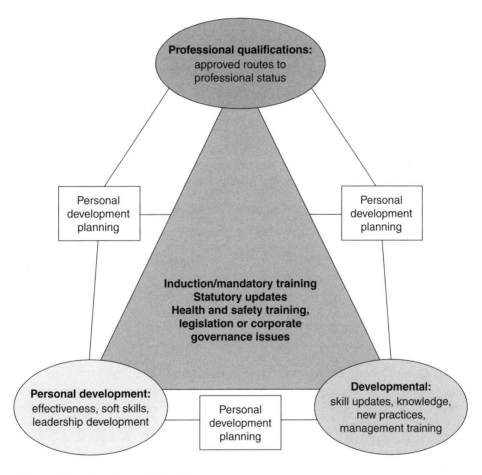

Figure 5.4: Developing CPD pathways.

Exercise 14: Developing in-house training sessions

In-house training sessions can be a cost-effective way of training staff, particularly if staff are working part time or some team members do not have access to transport. Anyone involved in the design or delivery of an event can refer to this simple checklist (Box 5.6) to ensure that the main components of an effective session are included.

Quick reference guide to Exercise 14

🕐 = 15 minutes (used as quick checklist)

☺ = No facilitation required

① = Simple and straightforward

There are several ways to organise in-house training.

* Training organisations such as the Red Cross or occupational health departments can run first-aid or resuscitation sessions in-house, for instance. Check out what generic training providers can do for you before designing your own session. Their expertise could save you time and money.
* Work with training providers to develop specific programmes for identified needs and deliver them internally using appropriate training methods. Produce detailed training specifications that clearly identify learning outcomes, training methods and evaluation requirements.
* Design sessions using internal resources and expertise as far as possible. Use the same approach detailing learning outcomes, methods and evaluation etc.

If you choose one of these options you should find the following checklist in Box 5.6 helpful. These simple points can help to ensure that a productive session is delivered. The checklist can also help to select a competent training provider, as these are the minimum requirements with which all professional trainers should be able to comply.

Box 5.6: Checklist for designing in-house training sessions

- Learning objectives (what the learners will get from the training) should be written against every identified training need.
- A programme for the event detailing the range and depth of the content, timings and training methods used should be produced.
- Consider external facilitation? If the content is specialised or complex you may require the help of specialists. They may be involved in the design and delivery of the session.
- Content should be a good balance of theory and practice and should be relevant to the organisation's culture and environment.
- A session plan detailing the main learning points, timings, methods and training aids should be produced and used.
- A suitable method of evaluation should be built into the event to measure the learning that has taken place and the outcomes.

Exercise 15: Training needs analysis

Identifying training needs is a generic task that everyone should be able to do. Table 5.11 takes a team or departmental view of training needs. It is useful for a team leader, supervisor or manager to use when putting together the annual training plan. Box 5.7 takes an individual view of the identification of training needs.

Quick reference guide to Exercise 15 (relevant to Table 5.11)
⏱ = One to two hours (part of the planning/review cycle)
☺ = No facilitation required
② = Level of difficulty related to size of team and complexity of change, identified need and skill mix required

---

Table 5.11   Drawing up the annual training plan

Department or team:			Date:
Key aspects of plan	*Healthcare area 1*	*Healthcare area 2*	*Healthcare area 3*
Service change required			
Expected benefit to patients			
People involved			
Training required			

Undertaking an individual's training needs analysis

> **Quick reference guide to Exercise 15 (relevant to Box 5.7)**
> ☉ = One to two hours (part of the planning/review cycle)
> ☺ = No facilitation required
> ② = Level of difficulty relates to seniority and complexity of roles and respon-
> sibilities

The form given in Box 5.7 should be completed after discussion between the individual and his/her line manager, based on an analysis of the department's or team's needs.

Box 5.7:   Drawing up an individual's training needs analysis

Name: Date: /   /

Which area of change am I involved in?

How does this affect my job and role(s)?

What training/support do I need to make the required changes?

Three objectives of the proposed training/development:

*

*

*

Who will provide the training?

When will it take place?

How much will it cost?

Signed: _____ Staff member

Signed: _____ Line manager

Exercise 16: Evaluation of learning – feedback questionnaire

A reflective evaluation questionnaire should be completed by everyone after every learning activity/training event. You might include the questions in Box 5.8 or other similar ones.

Quick reference guide to Exercise 16

🕐 = Five minutes

☺ = No facilitation required

① = Simple and straightforward

Box 5.8:   Feedback questionnaire

Post of respondent:

1   Were the aims and objectives of the event clearly
     stated in the initial information about the event?   Yes   No

     If NO, please give details:

2   Did the event meet your expectations?   Yes   No

     If NO, please give details:

3   Was the environment appropriate for the learning
     activity (e.g. room, seating arrangements,
     sound levels, external noise)?   Yes   No

     If NO, please give details:

4   Was the learning message clearly communicated?   Yes   No

     If NO, please give details:

5   Was your preferred style of learning catered for
     during the event?   Yes   No

     If NO, please give details:

6   Please tell us one thing you learned from this event:

continued opposite

7   In what way could the learning event be improved?

8   What benefits do you expect from this learning
     event (to you, patient care, the NHS)?

Free comments
In future programmes it would be good to ...

You could do less of ...

During the programme I most enjoyed the ...

Additional comments:

Evaluation

Evaluation of the outcomes of learning is seen as something which should be done but often is not, as it is difficult to measure the effectiveness of education and training. The modernisation agenda calls for evidence-based practice to become the norm and therefore organisations need to become more experienced at gathering evidence by evaluation.

Simple 'happy sheets', only rating superficial aspects of the event, should not be used any more. Lifelong learning requires people to evaluate the changes in their practice and behaviours to measure the effectiveness of their learning. Evaluation should be a continuous process covering all learning activity, not just formal training on a course.

A model that is particularly helpful in understanding how to measure learning outcomes is given in Figure 5.5. It illustrates the levels of evaluation of Kirkpatrick's hierarchy in relation to the measurement of meaningful learning for the learner and the organisation. This depth of evaluation can help the learning organisation to understand how learning directly affects behaviour and improves performance.

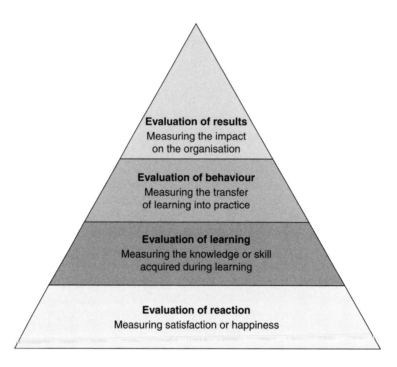

Figure 5.5:   Measuring learning outcomes (adapted from Kirkpatrick's hierarchy[3]).

Exercise 17: Checklist for research and development (R&D) partnerships (clinical and non-clinical research)

The checklist of this exercise can assist you in the initial planning of R&D projects that offer learning opportunities to partnerships. The exercise covers the basic and obvious points that need to be agreed between partners before entering into joint research projects. Table 5.12 illustrates the key stages and issues and encourages you to compare what is happening in your organisation against best practice. Tables 5.13 and 5.14 are templates for planning a research project and highlight key issues for consideration.

Quick reference guide to Exercise 17

🕐 = 10 to 50 hours (part of the planning cycle)

☺ = Some facilitation required to provide objectivity and challenge

③ = Level of difficulty relates to the nature of the research partnership, complexity of topic, scope of the project and availability of specialist skills and knowledge

---

Table 5.12   Key stages and issues for a learning organisation which is preparing an R&D proposal with partners

Stage or issue	Status
Clearly identified issue affecting multi-professions/multi-organisations	
Literature review	
Partner organisations/teams identified: lead person from each identified	
Research question agreed between partners	
Common objectives and outcomes agreed between partners (including equity/parity of the partnership, communication flows and trust and integrity of the research bid)	
Timescales agreed	
Funding sources identified	
Research bid written. Issues include: dealing with culture/subcultures, hierarchies, power bases, professional boundaries/tribalism, valuing diversity and future challenges	
Consideration of ethics issues	

continued overleaf

Table 5.12 *continued*

Stage or issue	Status

**You must apply to an NHS research ethics committee (REC)
when your research involves:**
- NHS patients, i.e. those subjects recruited by virtue of their past or
  present treatment by the NHS including those treated under contract
  with the private sector
- foetal material and in-vitro fertilisation involving NHS patients
- the recently dead in NHS premises
- access to records of past and present NHS patients
- the use of, or potential access to, NHS premises or facilities
  (including NHS staff)

Write and submit ethics forms (for advice *see* http://www.corec.org.uk)

Partner organisations' resources identified and pledged

Partner and host organisations' R&D approval sought and given –
responsibilities for host set out in the 'Research Governance Framework for
Health and Social Care' (http://www.doh.gov.uk/research/rd3/nhsrandd/
researchgovernance/govhome.htm)

Undertake the research

Evaluation/statistical analysis of the research project

Dissemination of the results

Implementation of research findings

Learning organisations should be actively involved in learning partnerships
that traverse professional or organisational boundaries, as they broaden their
perspectives and develop a deeper understanding of the shared environment.
    Tables 5.13 and 5.14 offer a simple framework for planning an R&D project.

Table 5.13   Research project initiation sheet

Topic or issue	Detail
Research project title	
Project lead(s)	
Project aim	

continued opposite

Table 5.13 *continued*

Topic or issue	Detail
Project objectives	•
	•
	•
	•
	•
	•
Project boundaries (what will and will not be covered)	
Key texts that inform research project	
People involved	(List by name and skill/knowledge/experience they bring)
Project outline	(A concise outline of the scope of the project, resources required and timescales involved)

Table 5.14   Research project planning sheet

Item	Detail	Timescale and people
Tasks		
Ethics and R&D considerations		
Resources		
Processes		
Implementation		
Evaluation		
Date of commencement	Signed	Project lead

References

1 Honey P and Mumford A (1986) *Using Your Learning Styles*. Peter Honey, Maidenhead.

2 Chambers R, Drinkwater C and Boath E (2003) *Involving Patients and the Public: how to do it better* (2e). Radcliffe Medical Press, Oxford.

3 Kirkpatrick DJ (1967) Evaluation of training. In: R Craig and J Bittel (eds) *Training and Development Handbook*. McGraw-Hill, New York.

6

Establishing a learning organisation in primary care

The last decade has been a time of great change for primary care. General practices have moved from relatively independent groups with a strong hierarchy of general practitioners to more interdependent practice groups linked within primary care organisations. Primary care organisations have four key objectives:

- primary care development and delivery
- commissioning services for the local population
- health improvement
- providing community services.

The changing environment has been chaotic for many practices, especially those without a well-developed infrastructure in IT capability or care pathways.

Ninety-nine per cent of people in England are registered with a GP. On average, five million people in the UK visit a GP each week. There are 635 000 district nurse consultations and 317 000 consultations with health visitors each week. Walk-in centres still see comparatively few patients with an average of 590 attendances each week. About four-fifths of patient contacts are made within general practice and yet only one-fifth of the NHS annual budget of £8.3 billion is spent on general practice. Patient surveys show that patients are generally happier with the clinical care that they receive, compared with the practice's organisation of services.[1]

The primary care workforce

There were nearly 26 000 whole time equivalent (WTE) GPs (unrestricted principals) working in the NHS in England in 2001, compared to just over 11 000 practice nurses working in general practices. In addition there are just over 10 000 WTE health visitors and nearly 11 000 WTE district nurses working in England. The ratio of practice nurses to GPs is 1 to every 2.3 GPs

– very different from the hospital sector where there is an average of four nurses to every doctor.

There has been little growth in the numbers of GPs since 1996 – insufficient to absorb the expanding workload for GPs and replace the numbers of GPs retiring. The numbers of district nurses are plummeting – there were nearly 1000 fewer district nurses in 2001 compared to 1995. A recent report by the Audit Commission recommended that a national strategy is needed to promote nursing careers in general practice and to develop nurse practitioners.[1]

Box 6.1:   Variations in service provision

A recent report by the Audit Commission praised many aspects of general practice, especially patient satisfaction with clinical care. General practice outperforms hospitals in levels of patient satisfaction, despite having less than 10% of the NHS budget.

The report highlighted variations in general practice care, such as the geographic differential in per capita expenditure on the number of patients per head of population and the variation in statin prescribing rates, that are not explicable on the basis of differences in need.[1]

The definitions and frameworks for general practitioners with special interests (officially abbreviated as GPwSIs) preserve the doctor's generalist expertise while including training and expertise in a specific area. The initial 11 areas for development include: cardiology, elderly care, diabetes, palliative care and cancer, mental health, dermatology, musculoskeletal medicine, women/child/ sexual health, ear/nose/throat, care for homeless/asylum seekers/travellers, and other procedures such as endoscopy, cystoscopy and vasectomies.

There is significant interest in the extension of the pharmacist's role.[1] New approaches to workforce development include revising pharmacists' roles and responsibilities to encourage:

- continuing to extend their role in supporting patients taking prescribed medicines
- developing the role of pharmacy technicians and other support staff
- developing schemes in which a qualified pharmacy technician works within standard protocols to dispense and supply medicines without the personal supervision of a pharmacist.[2]

What does a primary care trust that is a learning organisation look like?[3]

A PCT that is a learning organisation has a sound logical base for encouraging learning and an internal culture of learning, audit, critical enquiry and research. This includes the following features:

- a conceptual framework integrating the individual's learning activities with the organisation's learning, directed at patient care
- positive development of a culture in which learning is valued and enabled
- opportunities for multiprofessional learning that are tied into strategic outputs (clinical governance, National Service Frameworks, best practice)
- education and training that is based on adult educational principles
- a workforce who are enabled to develop insight into learning needed to achieve optimal health outcomes for their patient populations.

A PCT learning organisation will have an educational framework which has:

- a cascade of tutors from all disciplines working between the PCT management and grassroots workforce
- workforce planning that is an integral part of the policy and plans for education and training, so that meaningful links between undergraduate and postgraduate education result in relevant curricula at all stages of new developments
- a regular (at least annual) overall assessment of learning needs from an organisational perspective, mapping all the learning activities within the trust's constituency and what is available outside, and identifying gaps in knowledge and skills – from individuals' appraisals and from dedicated needs assessments that are topic and service based
- funding allocation arrangements to reflect service priorities
- positive activities that overcome barriers to the vision of a learning organisation – especially those that obstruct the incorporation of lay input and multiprofessional learning
- evaluation at all stages of the quality and relevance of planning, delivery and outputs in a performance assessment framework, which subsequently feeds back into the revision of the educational strategy.

A PCT learning organisation will:

- provide strong leadership
- value investment in education and training as a way to enhance the quality of healthcare and the staff's morale and motivation
- make the delivery of sufficient education and training possible to meet the identified needs, based on best adult educational principles

- invest in the research and development of education
- allow the PCT to continue growing as a learning organisation that meets society's expectations
- work and learn with neighbouring PCTs, other health organisations and educational bodies to enhance everyday practice.

The Modernisation Agency of the DoH has described the personal and organisational competencies expected of board members of PCTs in the following theme areas: organisational maturity, primary care, service provision, securing service delivery, partnership, health improvement, community engagement, clinical quality and workforce matters. The National Primary Care Trust Development Team offers training and development to PCTs for these theme areas.

Workforce retention and morale

Listening to staff and empowering them, establishing high quality CPD for all, and adopting a thoroughly integrated approach to managing the workforce were three of the key messages about remedying the nursing shortage in a work published by the King's Fund.[4]

An interview study of ex-nurses who had left the NHS found a variety of reasons to explain why they left, which spanned:

- lack of career progression
- limited professional development
- resistance to service improvements
- non-family-friendly working patterns
- bullying, inflexible, hierarchical management
- poor morale
- dangerous or inadequate staff–patient ratios
- increased patient activity resulting in poorer care
- lack of resources to meet identified needs
- a 'make do' culture
- poor working conditions
- pay not commensurate with responsibility and autonomy
- excessive caseloads
- difficulty in influencing decisions
- quality of care ignored
- poor team spirit.[5]

Occupational healthcare services for the one million or so in the NHS workforce are patchy and only readily available to a minority of workers in primary care. The government has recently reminded primary care trusts of their obligation to establish occupational healthcare for those working in primary care. In the past, many employers within the NHS have viewed inability to cope with stress as a failing of the employee, for which the individual concerned should be responsible. They have not recognised that organisational pressures have contributed to that employee suffering from stress and that, as employers, they have organisational and corporate responsibilities. The employer has a legal duty to take an interest in the causes of stress and primary prevention, as well as treatment and rehabilitation of any of their employees suffering from ill-health arising from work-related stress. Stress is multifactorial in terms of causes and outcomes. The management of systems and processes within the practice, trust or primary care organisation is key to preventing or reducing stress and pressures for their employees. The performance of individuals is affected both by the individuals themselves and the environment.

Promoting the job satisfaction of staff is increasingly being acknowledged as important by managers in healthcare. Job satisfaction links with the quality of services and care as a whole. In one study of 81 general practices, those with low job demands were twice as likely to have medium to high job satisfaction as those with high job demands.[6] Those with high job control were almost ten times more likely to have medium to high job satisfaction than those with low control over their job. Similarly, those with high social support were almost ten times more likely to report medium to high job satisfaction compared with those with low levels of support. Receptionists, practice nurses, district nurses and health visitors had lower job satisfaction than doctors – probably because they had lower levels of control and/or support at work. It seems that clinical autonomy is a more important determinant of job satisfaction for medical professionals than managerial autonomy.[7] Increases in the volume or complexity of work will not necessarily lead to lower job satisfaction if changes are accompanied by increased opportunities for doctors and others to control how their work is accomplished – for example, by delegation or flexible working.

Implementing clinical governance within primary care

Clinical governance is becoming embedded in the everyday life of general practice teams as continuing quality improvement and is generally seen as a positive process. However, 'a considerable body of evidence suggests that there are real concerns about the time, effort and personal sacrifices involved in developing the process at a local level'.[8]

Embedding clinical governance in the culture of primary care developments at practice level will therefore require sustained support from the primary care organisation, which in turn requires continuing support and guidance from the Department of Health.

> 'Successful implementation of clinical governance will require an understanding of the need for multi-level approaches to change, directed at the individual (e.g. GP), the group or team (e.g. primary health care team), the overall organisation (e.g. the primary care organisation) and the larger system (e.g. the NHS) in which individuals and organisations are embedded.' [8]

Another recent study concluded that 'senior primary care managers responsible for implementing clinical governance place a high priority on the need to change the culture of general practice to one that is more focused on accountability, collaboration between practices, and reflective learning. There are significant historical, structural, political and professional barriers to facilitating or managing this change'.[9]

Anticipating the future

Teaching PCTs

Teaching PCTs will be expected to promote a multidisciplinary workforce through education and training, and trialling and evaluating different models of working.

They will be advocating a lifelong culture of learning for health professionals – and patients. Joint initiatives between universities, Workforce Development Confederations and Teaching PCTs will:

- increase the quantity and quality of undergraduate and postgraduate training in primary care
- ensure continuing professional development by implementing training programmes for all staff
- develop the potential for patients to use primary care as a learning environment
- develop the potential of e-learning
- improve workforce planning to increase the recruitment and retention of staff
- develop partnership working at an inter-professional level
- support service development within an educational and research framework.[10]

Implementing the NSFs

PCTs are managing the greater emphasis on accountability and uniformity of standards in general practices with the implementation of the National Service Frameworks (NSFs). They are very aware of the need to ensure that they synchronise their work programmes in implementing each of the NSFs and other national priorities. Practices and PCTs need to find generic ways of working that fulfil the requirements of several NSFs simultaneously through:

- developing good information systems – appropriate computer capability in practices, training, consistent data entry
- health improvement and disease prevention – prioritising areas of greatest benefit where there is evidence of effective interventions and likely behaviour change; promoting healthy lifestyles opportunistically and in targeted ways; building on others' initiatives and resources
- addressing inequalities and reaching the 'hard to reach' groups in the population – good quality data about the local population; targeting health promotion in culturally appropriate ways; using innovative modes of communication
- screening and case finding of those in the high risk groups – for single and multiple diseases
- chronic disease management – managing in the primary care setting as far as possible; empowering patients to improve their self-care; involving pharmacists
- referrals – using all members of the primary care team appropriately, including specialist GPs and nurses.[11]

Redesigning the primary care workforce

The Wanless Report[12] warns that the UK must devote a significantly larger proportion of its national income to healthcare over the next 20 years. The rise is due to the anticipated health needs of the population, rising patient and public expectations, technology and medical advances, the use of the workforce and other productivity changes.

Coping with these changes will mean being more imaginative in workforce planning about new roles and ways of working in primary care. For instance, in an initiative to model future services to people over the age of 65 years, it was reckoned that 50% of the extra workload could be absorbed by growth in primary care nursing with better co-ordination with community services to maintain more people in their own homes. Non-professional, trained staff could be employed to reduce demand on increased numbers of health professionals and their corresponding individual workloads.[13]

The new GP contract

The new GP contract will link quality improvement and resources in general practices. GPs will be rewarded for the quality of services they provide for patients as a graded scheme based on incentives and rewards. The new arrangements should allow GPs to control their workloads and the skill mix of their practice team.[14]

References

1   Audit Commission (2002) *A Focus on General Practice in England.* Audit Commission, Wetherby.

2   Department of Health (2002) *Pharmacy Workforce in the New NHS. Making the best use of staff to deliver the NHS Pharmacy Programme.* Department of Health, London.

3   Chambers R (ed.) (2000) *Primary Care Trusts as Learning Organisations – the NHS Alliance view.* NHS Alliance, Retford.

4   Meadows S, Levenson R and Baeza J (2000) *The Last Straw: explaining the NHS nursing shortage.* King's Fund, London.

5   National Association of Primary Care (2001) *Medical and Nursing Workforce Survey.* NAPC, London.

6   Calnan M, Wainwright D, Forsyth M *et al.* (2000) *Health and Related Behaviour Within General Practice in South Thames.* Centre for Health Services Studies, University of Kent, Canterbury.

7   Sibbald B, Enzer I, Cooper C *et al.* (2000) GP job satisfaction in 1987, 1990 and 1998: lessons for the future? *Fam Pract.* **17 (5)**: 364–71.

8   Campbell S and Sweeney G (2002) The role of clinical governance as a strategy for quality improvement in primary care. *BJGP Quality Supplement.* **52**: S12–S17.

9   Marshall M, Sheaff R, Rogers A *et al.* (2002) A qualitative study of the cultural changes in primary care organisations needed to implement clinical governance. *BJGP.* **52**: 641–5.

10   Heads of Departments of General Practice and Primary Care in the Medical Schools of the United Kingdom (2002) *New Century, New Challenges.* Department of General Practice, University of Glasgow, Glasgow.

11   Department of Health (2002) *National Service Frameworks. A practical aid to implementation in primary care.* Department of Health, London.

12   Wanless D (2002) *Securing our Future Health: taking a long-term view.* Public Enquiry Unit, London.

13   Schofield M (chair of National Steering Group) (2002) *The Future Healthcare Workforce.* Chamberlain Dunn Associates, Richmond-upon-Thames.

14   General Practitioners Committee (2003) *New GMS Contract. Investing in General Practice.* British Medical Association, London.

7

Individualising learning organisations for secondary care

The nature of secondary care organisations

What is a hospital? If it were a collection of more or less dilapidated buildings then the NHS would be in a poor state indeed! A hospital is predominantly the people who work within those dilapidated buildings: their skills and dedication. Secondary care organisations are complex, large structures, which are organised along hierarchical lines (*see* Figure 7.1). Everyone on the planet may only be six handshakes from the President of the United States, but there is likely to be five tiers of management between a worker on the ward and the hospital

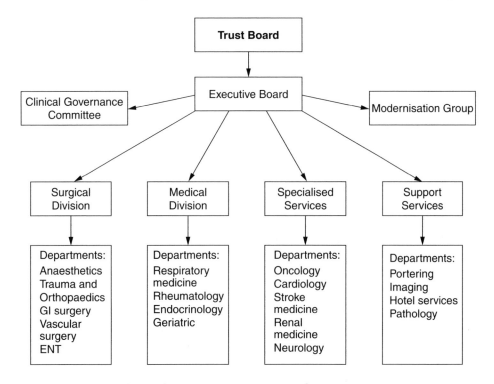

Figure 7.1:   Typical secondary care trust organisation chart.

trust board. It is no surprise that most staff members of a hospital trust would be hard-pressed to name the Chair of their trust.

'Must dos'

Above the hospital management structure sits the Department of Health hierarchy with many levels of bureaucracy leading to the Secretary of State for Health (*see* Figure 7.2). The Department of Health issues orders to the organisation, usually in the form of Executive Letters. Within these are 'must dos' – things that are an absolute requirement from the Department of Health. Examples of 'must dos' are waiting times for outpatients, the number of cancelled operations and trolley waits in casualty. Failure to deliver on 'must dos' will jeopardise the job of the chief executive of the trust. In order to achieve 'must dos' the chief executive will lean on his/her management team with an implicit and sometimes explicit threat to their careers. Learning has to be instilled within this climate of a command structure focused on short-term aims.

Figure 7.2:   Department of Health hierarchy.

How do education and training fit in?

The general pressures of service delivery on the management structure and staff are pitted against the training and development of staff – all are competing imperatives. The majority of medical staff within a hospital are in 'training grades'. Programmes like 'Investors in People' and the importance of human resources departments within management structures are evidence of the commitment the NHS has to its staff.

Workforce Development Confederations

In March 1999 the House of Commons Health Select Committee recommended that there be reorganisation of workforce planning in the NHS. The government set out the following principles to govern the reorganisation.[1]

- The NHS and the NHS Executive must be clear about service needs and the skills and staff required to deliver those services efficiently and effectively.
- Thinking about services, workforce and resources should be considered together to ensure that plans and developments are consistent and co-ordinated.
- There should be an appropriate mix between central (top-down) and local (bottom-up) planning.
- Planning should cover the whole healthcare workforce, looking across sectors (primary, secondary and tertiary), employers (public, private and voluntary) and staff groups (nurses, doctors, dentists, other professions and other staff) and should take account of evolving roles.
- Workforce planning arrangements should reflect clear and agreed responsibilities and accountabilities, with effective performance management systems.

Twenty-four Workforce Development Confederations (WDCs) have been established in England. The Department of Health spends almost £3 billion on training. The WDCs have a central role in enabling the delivery of the strategic health authorities' plans through the training of the workforce within the NHS. A business plan agreement between the strategic health authority (StHA) and the WDC will set out the functions to be undertaken by the WDC to support the delivery of the SHA. A business plan agreement between the WDC and the postgraduate deanery will set out those functions to be undertaken by the deanery in partnership with the WDC's workforce plans.

Workforce Development Confederations are partnership organisations comprising both NHS and non-NHS member organisations who need to work closely with the strategic health authorities and the postgraduate deaneries to

---

Box 7.1:   A Workforce Development Confederation's membership is drawn from:

- ambulance trusts
- strategic health authorities
- NHS trusts
- primary care trusts
- postgraduate deaneries
- care trusts.

The wider membership includes:

- councils with social services responsibilities and other social care employers
- further education institutions
- higher education institutions
- independent sector organisations
- Learning and Skills Councils
- Ministry of Defence
- National Blood Authority
- NHS Direct
- prison service
- voluntary sector organisations.

---

deliver on workforce issues in the context of the NHS Plan and local priorities (see the lists of those included in Box 7.1).

WDCs will ensure that all practice learning environments are:

- suitable learning environments offering opportunities to facilitate multi-disciplinary learning
- available in sufficient numbers to meet the training needs of the service
- managed, supervised and assessed by appropriately experienced and qualified professional staff
- quality assured and responsive to student evaluation and feedback.

Box 7.2:   Example of training needs resulting from service delivery

In order to have beds available for patients who had undergone neurosurgical operations and also to increase the hospital's capacity for high dependency care, a Neurosciences High Dependency Unit (NHDU) was developed.

An area was identified on a neurosurgical ward, which was refurbished to high dependency standards. An operational policy was developed. A training plan identified the need to train up the existing staff on the ward in intensive care techniques. Members of the existing staff should have been released for two days a week to go to the intensive care unit in order to be taught how to manage critically ill patients. Due to staff shortages and pressure of work, staff

continued opposite

---

were not released in sufficient numbers or for enough time. At the time of opening of the NHDU there were insufficient staff to both work on the ward and the NHDU, and staff expressed a reluctance to work in the NHDU as they felt that they lacked the appropriate skills.

A nurse with senior management skills was seconded to run the ward and the NHDU. Intensive-care-trained nurses were seconded to the NHDU to provide both training and psychological support to the existing staff. A recruitment drive was undertaken to bring nursing numbers on the ward and on the NHDU to establishment levels. Two of the four beds on the NHDU were closed until they could be safely nursed.

Lessons learned were:

- service developments need to be backed by a robust training plan for the staff involved
- the demands of service provision should not be allowed persistently to undermine the delivery of such training
- clinical leadership is essential in the implementation of training plans and service developments.

Doctors working in secondary care

Most medical posts have contractual obligations for study leave and all training posts are subject to periodic review by the Royal Colleges to ensure that there is a balance between service delivery and training. However, if four SHOs (senior house officers) are off sick, remaining patients are piling up in the Medical Admissions Unit, and an outlying ward has not seen a doctor for 24 hours, it is likely that the junior manager will pressurise the remaining SHOs into not attending their half-day teaching so that they are free to take care of patients. Arguments about the need to train today's SHOs – otherwise there will be no SHOs to look after patients tomorrow – may get lost in the urgency of the moment.

The current method of training doctors

Historically, the training of doctors in general, and in secondary care in particular, has been based on an apprentice approach. Traditionally there has been little formal didactic teaching, but instead learning through doing, which has been encapsulated by the saying, 'See one, do one, teach one.'

The current method of training consultants goes through four phases: medical student, pre-registration house officer, senior house officer and specialist registrar (SpR) (*see* Figure 7.3). There are three organisational groups who control this training process: the General Medical Council (GMC), the Royal Medical Colleges and the deaneries (the educational arm of the Department of Health).

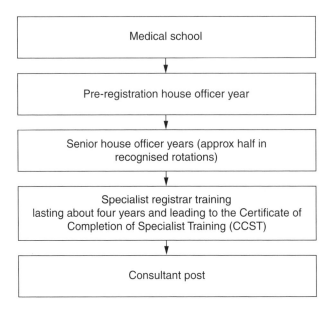

Figure 7.3:   Current development pathway for consultants

The GMC has a particular remit with regard to ensuring that doctors are safe to practise. It exercises control over the medical schools and the pre-registration house officer year. That year is a prerequisite to obtaining medical *registration* for junior house officers: that is, to have their names put on the GMC's register of doctors.

Box 7.3:   Example entry in General Medical Council register (http://www.gmc-uk.org/)

Registration number	2781770
Name:	Ellis, Simon Jonathan
Postal town:	Stoke-on-Trent
Provisional registration date:	30/12/1982
Full registration date:	01/02/1984
Qualifications:	BChir 1982, MB 1983 Camb
Specialist indicator:	SR
Sex:	Male

The Royal Medical Colleges inspect and recognise posts as being suitable for training. They also run the professional examinations such as the examination for Membership of the Royal College of Physicians (MRCP). Passing these examinations is necessary in order to progress to the SpR grade, and in surgical specialties, exit examinations (examinations at the end of the SpR training) have also been developed. Pass rates for Royal College Part II examinations range from 28% to 79%. These examinations are not subject to any external quality assurance and there has been no comprehensive review of the college examination system and how fit the examinations are for their supposed purpose.

Box 7.4: Dates of the College Charters

Royal College of Surgeons of Edinburgh	1505
Royal College of Physicians of London	1518
Royal College of Physicians and Surgeons of Glasgow	1599
Royal College of Physicians of Ireland	1654
Royal College of Physicians of Edinburgh	1681
Royal College of Surgeons in Ireland	1784
Royal College of Surgeons of England	1800
Royal College of Obstetricians and Gynaecologists	1930
Faculty of Dental Surgery	1947
Royal College of General Practitioners	1952
Royal College of Pathologists (College 1963)	1970
Royal College of Psychiatrists (Society 1841)	1971
Royal College of Radiologists (Faculty 1939)	1975
Faculty of Public Health Medicine	1978
Faculty of Occupational Medicine	1978
Royal College of Anaesthetists (Faculty 1948)	1992
Royal College of Ophthalmologists (Society 1880)	1988
Royal College of Paediatrics and Child Health	1996

The deaneries, through the regional postgraduate deans, hold the budgets for junior doctor training and also inspect posts as being suitable for training.

In the recent past, the registrar grade was reformed, from an unstructured and unlimited time working as a registrar and then a senior registrar, to a single grade of SpR with a structured training programme and periodic assessments.

Contrast between the United Kingdom and the United States

The culture within the NHS for the past 50 years has been primarily directed to service delivery with too few resources. There has been an element of complacency within the organisation as a result of the belief that the NHS was 'the best in the world'. British doctors have generally thought of themselves as being among the best doctors in the world. What they lacked in terms of technology they thought they compensated for by clinical acumen, developed through vast exposure to patients. What had not been fully appreciated was that in order to benefit from that clinical exposure there has to be sufficient time to reflect on, and review, the published literature. In a typical American teaching hospital with residents (trainee grade doctors), patients admitted would be discussed among the residents on a daily basis and the more senior residents would provide photocopies of relevant trials or review documents to their more junior residents. Within the British system recourse to the literature is the exception and usually reserved for specialised grand rounds or weekly case presentations.

The proposed method of training doctors

A radical reorganisation of medical training has been proposed by Sir Liam Donaldson, Chief Medical Officer for England, in *Unfinished Business: proposals for reform of the senior house officer grade*.[2] In these proposals, the house officer year is to be expanded to two years and the somewhat unstructured SHO years are to be reformed into a Basic Specialist Training Programme lasting two to three years (*see* Figure 7.4). Eight specialist training programmes are proposed (*see* Box 7.5) and each of these programmes will be organised through the postgraduate dean's office.

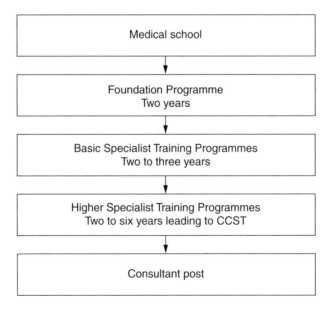

Figure 7.4:   Proposed development pathway for consultants.

Box 7.5:   Basic Specialist Training Programmes

- Medicine in General.
- Surgery in General.
- General Practice.
- Child Health.
- Mental Health.
- Obstetrics and Gynaecology.
- Pathology in General.
- Anaesthetics in General.

Implications for secondary care organisations

The planned changes to junior doctors' training posts will have a significant impact on secondary care organisations in that a large proportion of their medical workforce will become less committed to service provision and more directed to training and education. Hospitals which fail to adjust to these changes with improvements in the educational content of SHO posts will find their posts taken away when those posts are reorganised into Basic Specialist Training Programmes.

In recognition of the imperative to improve training within secondary care, educationalists have been appointed to senior management positions. One model being tried is to have a deputy medical director responsible for education and training and to have directors of the various programmes answerable to him/her (*see* Figure 7.5).

The management structure for training programmes and the training programmes themselves cut across specialist and directorate boundaries. This presents problems of accountability. The Head of Division for Medicine may feel understandably aggrieved if the Director of the Medicine in General programme, who happens to be a renal physician, removes an SHO from the medical wards to the renal ward as the educational experience there is perceived to be superior. This is why access to a deputy medical director who is working closely with the medical director allows educational priorities to receive their appropriate consideration.

Assessment of posts

Secondary care organisations will need to have a system of assessing their SHO posts for their educational content prior to external review by the deanery. There will also have to be the organisational commitment to change working practices in order to enhance educational quality even at the expense of a

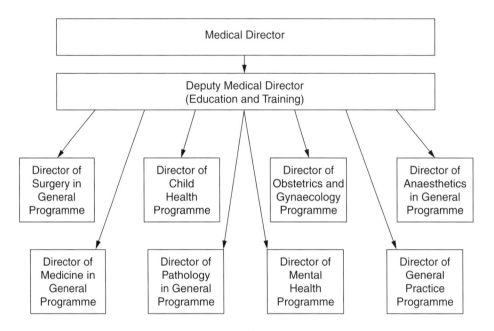

Figure 7.5. New secondary care education and training structure.

short-term reduction in service provision. An example of an assessment tool for rating the content of education and training in medical SHO posts is given in Box 7.6.

Nursing

The training and maintenance of competence for nurses and midwives is regulated by the Nursing and Midwifery Council (NMC), formerly the United Kingdom Central Council for Nursing, Midwifery and Health Visiting.

Pre-registration nursing programmes aim to teach:

- professional, ethical and legal issues
- the theory and practice of nursing
- the context in which health and social care is delivered
- organisational structures and processes
- communication
- social and life sciences relevant to nursing practice
- frameworks for social care provision and care systems.

Nursing programmes are based on the concept that nursing is a practice-based profession and are founded on the principles that:

- evidence should inform practice through the integration of relevant knowledge

Box 7.6: Assessment tool for SHO posts					
Post name:					
Date of assessment:					
Assessment performed by:					
Current post holder:					
	Excellent	Good	Acceptable	Needs improvement	Unacceptable
Consultant ward rounds (two a week minimum expected)					
Registrar support (at least daily)					
Workload (maximum 25 patients)					
On-call commitments					
Protected teaching time (half day a week)					
Attending outpatients (minimum once per week, ideal twice)					
Study leave available when needed					
External courses financed					
Educational supervision on firm					
Educational supervision on rotation					
Total					

- students are actively involved in nursing care delivery under supervision
- the *Code of Professional Conduct* applies to all practice interventions
- skills and knowledge are transferable
- research underpins practice
- lifelong learning and continuing professional development are important.

Once a nurse has qualified there is an ongoing requirement for continuing professional development.

Box 7.7:   The post-registration education and practice (PREP) standard

This standard is about the continuing professional development of registered nurses and midwives. To meet it, they must:

- undertake at least five days (35 hours) of learning activity relevant to their practice during the three years prior to their renewal of registration
- maintain a personal professional profile of this learning activity
- comply with any request from the NMC to audit compliance with these requirements.

Allied health professions (AHPs)

Allied health professions, such as physiotherapists and speech and language therapists, were formerly known as PAMS (professions allied to medicine). They are regulated by the Health Professions Council (HPC). The HPC is a new independent, UK-wide regulatory body responsible for setting and maintaining standards of professional training, performance and conduct for the 13 healthcare professions that it regulates (*see* Box 7.8). The HPC does not regulate doctors, nurses, dentists, pharmacists or opticians/optometrists.

Box 7.8:   The Health Professions Council regulates:

- arts, music and drama therapists
- chiropodists/podiatrists
- clinical scientists
- dieticians
- medical laboratory scientific officers (MLSOs)
- occupational therapists
- orthoptists
- prosthetists
- orthotists
- paramedics
- physiotherapists
- radiographers
- speech and language therapists.

In a similar way in which the General Medical Council works with the medical Royal Colleges and the British Medical Association, the HPC has links with the professional bodies representing the professional groupings within it. For example, the Chartered Society of Physiotherapy (CSP) is the professional, educational and trade union body for over 39 000 chartered physiotherapists, physiotherapy students and physiotherapy assistants working or training (or who have trained) in Britain. It is committed to the principles of continuous professional and personal development. The CSP maintains the following principles.

- The individual learner is responsible for managing and undertaking CPD activity and the effective learner knows best what he/she needs to learn.
- The learning process is continuous in a systematic cycle of analysis, action and review.
- Learning objectives should be clear and should serve organisational needs and patient needs as well as individual goals.
- The process is planned and based on identifiable outcomes of learning that the individual achieves.

These are sound objectives based on the principles of adult learning and could be signed up to by any professional.

Interdisciplinary training

There has been a theoretical commitment to interdisciplinary training, which may have a greater chance of realisation with the development of the Workforce Development Confederations.

Box 7.9:   Inter-professional education

Inter-professional education involves informal and formal opportunities for members of two or more professions to learn with and from each other, involving patients/users of health and social care where possible, with the aims of improving the effectiveness of care delivery and increasing collaborative practice.[3]

Box 7.10:   Best practice in inter-professional education

Inter-professional education should:

- reflect the needs and interests of the patient
- be derived from an integrated care approach
- complement profession-specific knowledge
- have its main focus in practice, supported by inter-professional learning in academic components of programmes
- allow practitioners clearly to identify and maintain their own philosophies of care, including their professional values and beliefs, within an inter-professional working environment.[3]

Quality assurance

Clinical governance

Some systematic method of getting an overview of quality assurance is particularly important for secondary care organisations, with their multidisciplinary workforces and complex organisational structures. Appropriate training of the workforce underpins a lot of clinical governance – as described in Box 7.11. The implementation of the clinical governance agenda is dependent on the existence of appropriately trained staff. For example, implementation of clinical risk management requires the training of staff in the recognition and minimisation of clinical risk.

Box 7.11:   Commitment and support to education, training and competence of staff

- Mechanisms are in place to facilitate staff to access clinical supervision and protected teaching time.
- Local induction programmes meet those set by the deanery, Royal Colleges and specialist training requirements.
- The training needs of staff are analysed and used to inform training programmes.
- Personal development plans are developed and implementation monitored in response to appraisal.
- Training records and the outcomes of training are monitored, including cascading of key information where appropriate.
- Mechanisms are in place to verify that all staff have access to appraisal and ensure that information from the appraisal process is used to identify training needs.
- Mechanisms are in place to ensure equity of access to training and that CPD is monitored within the directorate.

Continuing professional development

A requirement of clinical governance is that personal development plans are developed and implemented. To give some quality assurance to the type of continuing training that is occurring, various professional bodies have laid down criteria. The NMC has PREP and the medical Royal Colleges have various systems of continuing professional development. All healthcare workers should have a system of appraisal and a system of continuing professional development arising out of that.

Box 7.12:   The Royal College of Physicians' requirements for CPD accreditation[4]

The requirements for CPD are expressed in terms of credits, where one learning credit is gained by undertaking one hour of approved educational activity. Credit requirements are:

- a *minimum* of 50 education credits per year: 250 credits over five years. This should include 25 *non-clinical* education credits over five years.

Some of these systems have been criticised as being over-restrictive and being contrary to the principles of adult learning, which should be self-directed.

Restructuring with learning in mind

The NHS is constantly changing to meet shifts in the evidence base, patients' expectations and political dictates. The structures and working relationships within secondary care are fairly rigid, but change provides an opportunity for moving training and education up the agenda.

Box 7.13:   Restructuring of acute medicine – an example

Within a hospital trust and outside, within the larger health community, there was recognition that acute medical emergencies were not being managed in the most efficient and safe fashion. Prompted by reports from external reviewers, a systematic review of the management of acute medicine was undertaken. This resulted in:

- the streaming of patients into their subspecialties
- daily acute post-take ward rounds by consultants
- the appointment of two new consultants with particular responsibility for acute medicine
- the presence of senior doctors in the medical admissions unit
- the development of an acute admissions ward.

Some of these reforms were of educational benefit to the SHO on the medical rotation. There were increased opportunities for learning due to the greater supervision by seniors resulting from the post-take ward rounds and the consultants in the medical assessment unit. However, the educational component of SHO posts appeared to have taken second place to service considerations.

A committee was set up to review specifically the SHO posts from an educational point of view. All the posts were individually reviewed for their educational value. Some posts were recognised as being of poor educational value and were phased out. Other posts were improved by increasing the SHOs' exposure to outpatient

continued overleaf

clinics. Attendance at protected teaching time was monitored and, where particular directorates were not allowing SHOs to attend, the support of the medical director was sought and obtained.

- Restructuring of clinical services provides an opportunity for training developments.
- Specific provision needs to be made for educational requirements to be heard among the competing voices.
- Junior staff require educational champions to 'fight their corner'.

References

1   Department of Health (2002) *Workforce Development Confederation: functions, accountabilities and working relationships.* Department of Health, London.

2   Donaldson L (2002) *Unfinished Business: proposals for reform of the senior house officer grade.* Department of Health, London.

3   United Kingdom Central Council for Nursing (1999) *Fitness for Practice and Purpose: the report of UKCC's post-commission development group.* UKCC, London.

4   Royal College of Physicians of Edinburgh on behalf of the Royal Colleges of Physicians (2002) http://www.rcpe.ac.uk/CPD/CPD_scheme_details.html.

8

The role of patients in a learning organisation

A new era in public involvement is emerging with greater emphasis on transparency, openness, accountability and patient-focused services. The NHS Plan clearly indicated the intention to involve and consult patients and the general public about key issues within the NHS such as planning healthcare services, identifying local needs and priorities and evaluating the quality of services from a patient satisfaction viewpoint.[1] This has required a significant cultural shift within NHS professions.

Box 8.1: The government's view of the role of the patient – 'Patients will be in the driving seat'

'The needs of the patient will be central ... A modern and dependable national health service will ... be built around the needs of the people, not of institutions ...'[1]

'The Government expects health authorities to play a strong role in communicating with local people and ensuring public involvement in decision making about the local health service.'[2]

'Patients and carers need to be involved ... in their own care and in the planning, monitoring and development of health services ... making sure the NHS responds more quickly to patient needs.'[3]

'The NHS will shape its services around the needs and preferences of individual patients, their families and their carers ... Patients and citizens will have a greater say in the NHS, and the provision of services will be centred on patients' needs.'[1]

'By 2005 all patients and their GPs will be able to book appointments at both a time and place that is convenient to the patient ... Choice will also be underpinned by more information being provided to patients to help them make more informed choices ... patient power will be backed by new organisational arrangements ... statutory, independent Patient Forums in each trust, to monitor and review the quality of local services from a patient perspective ... These changes are all about shifting the balance of power towards patients in the NHS.'[4]

It could be argued that the patient has always been the focus of healthcare services but that this approach has often been coupled with a paternalistic attitude resulting in key decisions being made by health professionals on behalf of the patient. Clinicians and managers who have adopted a paternalistic approach have justified their actions by claiming that patients:

*   do not want the responsibility of making decisions
*   do not have the technical or medical knowledge to make informed decisions
*   have such confidence in the doctor–patient relationship that patients entrust significant health and medical decisions to the clinician(s) treating them.

With the increased access to health information and advice through the media and the internet, patients are now much more knowledgeable about their health and the treatments available to them. Many want to be given choices and to be involved in decisions about their care and treatment. As the general public are living to a greater age there is an emergent interest in health, lifestyle and wellbeing, and this is being reflected in the communication and involvement required by the public of the NHS. However, the review reported in Box 8.2 shows that clinicians need to be flexible about the extent of participation they assume patients want in making decisions about their own healthcare.

Box 8.2:   A systematic review of patients' preferred roles in decision making about their own healthcare

The review found that the most common preference of patients with *cancer and non-malignant diseases* was for a *passive* role in decision making about their clinical management, according to card scales. The most common preference of *healthy* participants was for an *active* role in decision making about healthcare choices. Older patients were less likely to want to participate actively in decision making than younger people; those with higher income levels and employed status had a more active preference and people from a lower socioeconomic group preferred a more passive role. Younger patients and healthy subjects and those with higher education levels are more likely to want to take a lead role in decision making.[5]

In learning organisations there is the ready recognition that a more equitable partnership between the organisation and its clients is required. Greater openness and accountability will strengthen public confidence and lead to a better understanding between healthcare professionals and service users. If any organisation is to succeed, it has to deliver the service that its customers need, in the way they want it delivered. This means that patients and the public have to interact with those working in the NHS in different ways, to educate members of the workforce about their specific requirements. This approach also gives the NHS an opportunity to influence public health generally by learning the most effective ways of educating target groups of the population about lifestyle, disease prevention and self-care for some chronic conditions. The NHS can build a stronger relationship with service users that expresses their confidence and trust in a service that is appropriately patient focused.

Learning organisations see three distinct ways in which patients, the public and healthcare providers can interact to enrich the learning culture:

* patients/public as teachers
* patients/public as learners
* patients/public as performance monitors.

Patients as teachers

The public can offer a valuable contribution, as users of the NHS, to the way in which services are configured, delivered and evaluated – *see* Box 8.3. It can be an enlightening experience for health professionals and managers to listen to those who access the service and therefore present an external view of how easy or difficult the service is to use.

Box 8.3: Patients can teach us about:

* how to improve accessibility and availability of services
* how patients' needs and requirements change and develop
* how to communicate effectively across all social and cultural groups, recognising special needs and requirements
* how the changing economic climate of the area affects patients' health services requirements
* what information is useful to patients for health education, specific conditions or prevention
* how to develop a user-friendly service that engenders trust and confidence.

Patient input is useful regarding how easy or difficult it is for them to access different forms of care and treatment. Patients can highlight if their rights are fully explained concerning access to medical records or choice over referrals to an NHS hospital trust or clinician.

If the modernisation of the NHS is to succeed, the reconfiguration of services should take into consideration the way in which work patterns change. Patients can support healthcare professionals by informing them of their changing requirements. Patients and the public can also share their personal experiences of the service to enable healthcare professionals and managers to develop a better understanding of their 'care' priorities. The views of people who do not currently access healthcare services, but who would like to or need to, are particularly useful. Clinic timings, the practicalities of walk-in centres and telephone advice need to be geared to the target population that accesses them regularly, even if that means healthcare professionals changing their working patterns to accommodate their patients' preferences. That is the duty of any service industry – public or private.

The way in which the NHS communicates with the public needs to be reviewed regularly to ensure that it is as effective as possible. By engaging members of the public in planning activities we can gauge how clear the message is. The NHS services a diverse population with varying cultural and religious backgrounds, physical impairments, mental health problems, vulnerabilities and special needs. Those should be reflected in the range of communication methods used. The truly effective way of measuring their impact is to involve those at whom the messages are aimed – as in the example given in Box 8.4 where health service researchers worked with South Asian and white patients with asthma.

Box 8.4:   Understanding user healthcare strategies – experiences of asthma therapy among South Asians and white cultural groups[6,7]

A qualitative study was undertaken with South Asian and white asthmatics and a sample of health professionals working with these groups. Respondents' narratives captured their compliance with medication, their use of alternative therapies and their relationships with health professionals. The analysis of the study demonstrated the importance of incorporating users' perspectives in the delivery of healthcare services to achieve better management of asthma.[6,7]

One area where there has been useful patient input into the National Health Service, resulting in learning for the NHS as a whole, has been via the disease-specific user groups. For example, the Multiple Sclerosis Society, stroke groups and the Neuropathy Trust all act as patient advocacy groups at local and national levels, as seen in Box 8.5.

Box 8.5:   Patient power – an example

The epilepsy group in North Staffordshire lobbied successfully to retain the service provided by an epilepsy specialist nurse and a similar lobbying process occurred for the multiple sclerosis service. Although the evidence base for specialist nurses is not well developed, patients appreciate them. Patient groups can affect priorities within the NHS via local political pressure.

At a national level it is doubtful whether the scheme to make beta-interferon available on the NHS to people with multiple sclerosis (MS) would have occurred but for the efforts of the MS Society. Patient groups can influence the direction of the NHS, but generally it is not through being invited in to consult on the direction of developments, rather via organised patient groups, who exist outside the NHS and who use tactics of political pressure to make the NHS listen.

The Expert Patient Programme recommends the active involvement of patients with designated chronic conditions to work with other patients and healthcare professionals to share information and first-hand experiences and develop self-management programmes. It is hoped that the development of such programmes will have a significant effect on the reduction in severity of the symptoms of patients with that particular chronic condition and will improve patients' confidence, resourcefulness and self-efficacy. The Expert Patients' Task Force cites evidence of benefits for the initiative of:

- reduced severity of symptoms
- significant decrease in pain
- improved life control and activity
- improved resourcefulness and life satisfaction.[8,9]

Box 8.6:　The Expert Patient Programme[9]

Launched in 2001 by the Chief Medical Officer, the Expert Patient Programme recommends the setting up of user-led groups. These enable people living with long-term medical conditions such as diabetes, asthma and arthritis to share their knowledge and skills to help other patients to better manage their conditions, to maintain their health and improve their quality of life.

'The new programme will help to create a new generation of patients who are empowered to take action with the health professional caring for them, e.g. to reduce pain, improve the use of medication and enhance their overall quality of life.'[8]

Another approach that is gaining in popularity throughout the NHS is that of 'peer education', especially for reaching vulnerable groups of people and modifying their behaviour. The example given in Box 8.7 illustrates the advantages of peer education for one disease area, coronary heart disease.

Box 8.7:　Peer education programme – Project Dil, Leicester

This Leicester-based project uses trained members of the community to work with a targeted population to reduce the risk factors for coronary heart disease. They have established a peer education health programme that supports local community members to work with peers directly and, through the development of health promotion materials, to improve morbidity and mortality.

　Further information about the project can be obtained from the project leader: Mina.bhavsar@leics-ha.nhs.uk.

A review of published literature about the role of patients as teachers found 13 journal articles reporting initiatives where patients taught physical examination skills, mostly musculoskeletal examinations. Nineteen articles described patients acting as 'assessors' of learners' performance, usually in a teaching programme. Reports from the NHS staff they had taught were all positive, many valuing the insights and confidence gained from practising skills on patients acting in a teaching role – as Box 8.8 shows. The authors concluded that 'involving patients as teachers has important educational benefits for learners. Patients offer unique qualities that can enhance the acquisition of skills and change attitudes towards patients'.[10]

Box 8.8:   Value of involving patients as teachers[10]

1   For NHS staff as learners:
- enables access to personal knowledge and experience of condition and use of services
- deepens understanding
- provides constructive feedback
- reduces anxiety
- increases confidence
- influences attitudes and behaviour
- improves acquisition of skills
- increases respect for patients
- places learning in context.

2   For patients acting as teachers:
- uses their disease or condition positively
- uses their knowledge and experience
- acknowledges their expertise
- creates a sense of empowerment
- provides an opportunity to help future patients
- increases their knowledge
- provides new insights
- improves their understanding of doctors.

3   For trainers:
- provides additional teaching resources
- improves quality of teaching
- offers alternative teaching opportunities
- develops mutual understanding
- enlists new advocates
- provides value for money.

Patients as learners

Organisations that have been slow to respond to public involvement often cite a lack of understanding and knowledge as a barrier to meaningful participation. There is no doubting the complexities of the NHS but involving users can help them to develop a better understanding of the challenges and difficulties professionals face when delivering care to diverse groups of patients.

The opportunity to involve patients as learners in a learning organisation is very exciting. They are exposed to issues of service delivery, logistics, rationing and resource management through the process of involvement. They could develop insight into the perennial problems of winter pressures, bed blocking and the importance of immunisation and flu vaccines as preventative measures. Such an arrangement would offer an opportunity to manage demand and build realistic expectations of the NHS on a long-term basis. The initiative described in Box 8.9 is one example of good practice where groups of people were successfully trained to lead public consultation initiatives.

Box 8.9: Educating the public to seek information about their own needs[11]

People over 65 years of age and people with sensory and mobility problems were trained to undertake consultation with others in their age group or with disabilities in an initiative in Stoke-on-Trent. Members of the group chose the topics of their consultation according to what *they* deemed to be priorities.

Topics included determining the public's knowledge about risks of stroke, barriers to disabled people being employed at work, and satisfaction with mobility aids and equipment. Lessons were also learned about setting up such an educational programme to train citizens to gain the perspectives of other members of the public about healthcare services.

Results were fed back to the sponsors in health and social services who realised:

- the benefits of empowering citizens from minority groups (such as older and disabled people) to determine the views of other people from those minority groups
- the problems encountered in training citizens in basic consultation skills
- the problems with current healthcare services and employment conditions.

Patients as 'learners' may also provide opportunities to introduce healthcare as a potential career option to groups of the population that have not traditionally considered the NHS as an employer.

Learning is a safe way to encourage patients to look at their actions and behaviours. Involving patients in the planning and evaluation of services they use may help to develop a culture of self-care, prevention and healthy lifestyles. By increasing their knowledge they may feel that they are more in control of their health and take greater responsibility for their health, so improving overall satisfaction.

Patients as performance monitors

The field of clinical governance has developed rapidly and has gained wide acceptance for being an effective quality improvement framework that identifies and manages risk at all levels of the organisation. Patients are expected to play an important role in evaluating service delivery and feeding back their views of effectiveness, satisfaction, openness and accessibility. These activities contribute to a better understanding of overall performance and health gain. As patients become more involved in the evaluation of services their confidence will grow, encouraging them to offer suggestions for improvements on access, information, patient care, delivery methods and future training needs.

The new legislation that followed the Bristol Inquiry[12] has strengthened the framework for high quality standards and accountability in the NHS. Patients' and the public's views and feedback about the quality and nature of services are part of the performance monitoring process. Being patient centred is one of the underpinning principles against which the Commission for Health Improvement (CHI) in England and Wales judges health services. The new Commission for Healthcare Audit and Inspection (CHAI) – the successor to CHI and the Audit Commission – will continue to seek patients' views as part of performance monitoring of trusts and undertake an independent scrutiny of patients' complaints – in public and private sectors. This commission will have a major role in explaining to the public how NHS resources have been deployed and the impact they have had in improving services, raising standards and improving the health of the nation.

On a local basis, patients and the general public take part in surveys undertaken by general practices, PCOs and hospital trusts. They are members of citizen panels who feed back views on specific questions and issues, posed by the panel sponsors. Lay people and non-executive directors are members of the boards of hospital and primary care trusts and strategic health authorities. They are champions of the public, who ensure that there is effective patient and public involvement – and who participate in the performance monitoring of the trusts' and authorities' work programmes.

Lay people will be part of the revalidation groups set up by the General Medical Council to monitor the quality of portfolios that doctors submit to verify that they are safe to practise. The portfolios that the revalidation groups will monitor and approve as being above minimum standards will include information from patient feedback about the doctor's performance. Other material will demonstrate the doctor's standards of practice and CPD learning cycles. There has been a long history of patients being involved in making judgements about general practice performance in the inspection process of training practices.

Public participation in decision making

By working together, health professionals' and the public's shared experience can inform a better understanding of local issues and improve methods of service delivery.

As health services become more patient centred, the views of members of the public will be valued at all stages of the provision of healthcare: planning and providing health services, evaluation and educating the workforce about patients' needs and preferences. Members of the public should be well informed about the issues so as to be on reasonably equal terms with decision makers.

Public participation will not be effective unless health professionals and managers welcome the contribution that the public and patients can make to decision making. If public participation is to be meaningful, those in authority need to be ready and willing to listen to the public's informed views about how the health service can be run so that it is appropriate for their needs, and to shift power and resources accordingly.

The stages of public participation

The terms 'participation', 'consultation' and 'involvement' tend to be used interchangeably in popular parlance in the NHS. However, 'participation' is used by others outside the NHS as the umbrella term that encompasses the progressively more participatory stages of:

1 information exchange – we give the public information, they give us information but we do not negotiate or develop a shared view
2 consultation – the public and patients express their views but those on the consultation team make decisions about developments
3 support – the public decides what to do and others support them in doing it
4 deciding together – the NHS, patients and the public thinking and planning together
5 acting together – the NHS, patients and the public putting plans into action together.[13]

'Involvement' is a rather vague term which is used to imply that some activity happened that brought the public or individual patients into contact with those working in the NHS to hear or receive views or information on a particular matter.

There are good examples of those working in primary care seeking patients' or the public's views, although the health service in the UK does not have a tradition of doing so in systematic or meaningful ways. The focus of patient participation in the past has often involved seeking patients' views on relatively trivial matters, such as the comfort of the waiting room or ease of making appointments. The views of people not seeking healthcare have rarely been sampled and the topics considered are usually relatively superficial, avoiding core aspects of the health service management or operation.

References

1   Secretary of State for Health (2000) *NHS Plan. A plan for investment. A plan for reform.* Department of Health, London.

2   Department of Health (1997) *The New NHS: modern, dependable.* Department of Health, London.

3   Department of Health (1996) *Patient Partnership: building a collaborative strategy.* Department of Health, London.

4   Secretary of State for Health (2002) *Delivering the NHS Plan. Next steps on investment. Next steps on reform.* Department of Health, London.

5   Jordan J, Chambers R and Ellis S (2003) To what extent do patients want to participate in decisions about their own health care? A systematic review. (Unpublished – to update.)

6   Gillam S and Brooks F (eds) (2001) *New Beginnings. Towards patient and public involvement in primary health care.* King's Fund, London.

7   Brooks F, Mitchell M and Lomax H (1999) *Managing Asthma: attitudes to asthma and asthma therapy among South Asian cultural groups. Research report no. 503.* University of Luton, Institute for Health Services Research, Luton.

8   Long-term Medical Conditions Alliance (LMCA) (2001) *Supporting Expert Patients.* LMCA, London.

9   Department of Health (2001) *The Expert Patient: a new approach to chronic disease management for the 21st century.* Department of Health, London.

10 Wykurz W and Kelly D (2002) Developing the role of patients as teachers: literature review. *BMJ.* **325**: 818–21.

11 Chambers R, Drinkwater C and Boath E (2003) *Involving Patients and the Public: how to do it better* (2e). Radcliffe Medical Press, Oxford.

12 Bristol Inquiry report is available on the web at http://www.bristol-inquiry.org.uk/final_report.

13 Taylor M (1995) *Unleashing the Potential. Bringing residents to the centre of regeneration.* Joseph Rowntree Foundation, York.

9

Make yours a learning organisation

If you have worked your way through the book you will (hopefully) have achieved several things.

- You will have a clearer understanding of what a learning organisation is and the beneficial effects that a learning culture can have on an organisation's effectiveness and its workforce.
- You will understand some of the key components that constitute a learning organisation.
- You will have recognised that a learning culture is a strong motivator for the workforce.
- You will have begun to form a plan of action to implement some of what you have read to bring about changes in the way your organisation uses learning to improve its effectiveness.

Learning organisations with properly managed corporate learning and continuing professional development bring about sustainable change, and benefit individuals, teams, the organisation and the wider world. Learning organisations have learned the secret of integration, whole-systems thinking and investment in their workforce. They understand that there is a significant difference between developing human resources and supporting resourceful humans. This basic understanding is what sets learning organisations aside from their more traditional counterparts.

The key messages are as follows.

- Understand the integration of a learning organisation; every action has a consequence somewhere.
- Standing back and seeing the whole picture gives the organisation greater flexibility in managing change, greater capacity to develop capability and improves recruitment, retention and staff morale.
- Empowerment of the workforce increases the power and effectiveness of the learning organisation.
- Shared learning that emanates from the centre of a learning organisation enables it to reinvent itself, to ride with changes and retain its effectiveness while more traditional organisations dissolve into chaos.

- A learning organisation needs a strong infrastructure to ensure that fair access, equal opportunities and shared learning take place.

It is important to recognise the reality as well as the ideal and many organisations will have elements of a learning organisation in place. However, they may need to establish whether there is enough commitment and support from their key decision makers to be able to create a learning organisation.

Table 9.1 outlines some of the variances that commonly exist in traditional healthcare organisations and some of the good practice that needs to be established to move towards a learning organisation.

Table 9.1:   Good practice and organisational reality for lifelong learning (adapted from Lewis and Whitlock 2002[1])

Lifelong learning descriptor	Good practice example	Organisational reality
Duration	• Encourage people to learn from everyday experience, to view each day as an opportunity for learning • Debrief after meetings/projects to assess individual/team learning • Debrief after training sessions to identify next learning steps for the individual/team • Build discussion of learning into performance reviews or appraisals • Discuss learning at times of change, e.g. promotion, retirement, redundancy	• Only structured learning formally recognised • Isolated, spasmodic learning episodes • Superficial evaluation at the end of training events • Learning viewed as remedial in appraisals or performance reviews • Learning matched to organisational timetable
Focus	• Develop trainers/managers as mentors/facilitators/coaches • Develop managers as role models of lifelong learners • Include personal learning/helping others to learn in competency frameworks	• People's development seen as being of secondary importance • Seen mainly as the training person's territory
Type/level of learning	• Find out what employees would like to learn • During performance reviews/ appraisals, focus on personal learning beyond immediate organisational needs • Run creative, off-the-wall events with a learning focus, e.g. volunteering in the community	• Learning decided by the organisation and management • Learning linked predominantly to achieving organisational objectives • Traditional learning usually with historical track record

continued opposite

Table 9.1: *continued*

Lifelong learning descriptor	Good practice example	Organisational reality
Access	• Open up/extend a learning centre; include some recreational learning resources • Provide opportunities for shadowing, job swaps, secondments • Provide personal learning entitlement (funds or days)	• Poorly resourced or completely outsourced • Usually available to select groups • Minimum standards for clinicians/nurses etc.
Learner choice	• Identify how employees like to learn (using a survey or focus group) • Employ a range of methods and resources to engage a wider audience • Develop learning partnerships with colleges/universities to accredit in-house training programmes for learners who wish to build up academic credits	• Organisation defines learning methods • Usually signposted externally • Learning partnerships dependent on local relationships; credits usually available for courses targeted at postgraduate levels

The important thing to consider is what you will do with the learning you have gained from considering the issues explored in this book. We hope that there has been a strong element of personal learning for you and would urge you to use the personal learning inventory (*see* Box 9.1) to reinforce your learning. You might use this inventory when you take time out to reflect on what you have achieved, looking back on a period of continuing professional development, and what you plan to learn about in future.

Box 9.1: Personal learning inventory

1 How will your learning influence your approach to:
   (a) lifelong learning

   (b) professional development

   (c) personal development?

2 How will learning influence your leadership and/or management of others?

continued overleaf

---

3   What are the most significant things you have learned from the issues explored in the period you are reviewing?

4   How will what you have learned change your behaviour?

5   What do you want to do differently in your current role?

Personal learning plan
I would like to learn more about ...

How I know that this topic(s) is a priority for me and the NHS:

What I would expect to gain is ...

What the organisation would expect to gain is ...

Specific learning objectives for the next x months:

Outcomes I desire from learning:

Outcomes I desire from applying learning in practice:

Resources required:

Timescales: Next steps (e.g. discuss and agree plan, identify resources etc.):

You may wish to influence a whole organisation to consider some of the suggestions and models we have outlined. This can be a difficult task and really needs a core group of committed enthusiasts or learning organisation champions to influence that level of organisational development so that something happens. Use the organisational learning inventory (*see* Box 9.2) to check the readiness, commitment and capacity of your organisation to adopt a learning culture.

Box 9.2: Organisational learning inventory

1   Does your organisation have the commitment and desire to establish a learning culture?

2   Which of the following criteria does your organisation have in place:
 (a)   clear vision of corporate learning being part of strategic planning activity
 (b)   clear statement of intent to support lifelong learning, CPD and reflective practice for all the workforce
 (c)   learning/education strategy and policies
 (d)   operational mechanisms that implement the policies
 (e)   lifelong learning and learning organisation champions with real power and influence
 (f)   identified and protected resources for learning and education
 (g)   evidence of shared learning with other organisations and partnerships?

What can I do to influence and/or inform my organisation of the potential of developing a learning organisation and/or learning culture?

Who can I contact that could help me to inform and influence others?

What are the first steps I need to take?

'Learning is a double loop ... there is learning to solve a particular problem and then, more importantly, there is the habit of learning, the learning to learn to do such things. That second loop can change the way you live.' (Charles Handy, *The Age of Unreason*)[2]

References

1   Lewis R and Whitlock Q (2002) Lifelong learning; a corporate perspective. *The Training Journal.* **May**: 14–18.

2   Handy C (1989) *The Age of Unreason.* Arrow, London.

Appendix 1

Further reading

- Argyris C (1992) *On Organisational Learning.* Blackwell, Oxford.
- De Geus A (1997) *The Living Company.* Nicholas Brealy, London.
- Pedler M, Borgoyne J and Boydell T (1991) *The Learning Company.* McGraw-Hill, London.
- Schon D (1987) *Educating the Reflective Practitioner.* Jossey-Bass, San Francisco.
- Senge P (1992) *The Fifth Discipline.* Century Business, London.
- Smith J and Spurling A (1999) *Lifelong Learning; riding the tiger.* Cassell, London.

Appendix 2

Useful websites

- **Bandolier** — www.ebandolier.com (evidence-based medicine e-journal)
- **British Medical Association (General Practitioners Committee)** — www.bma.org.uk (BMA site including GPC pages)
- **Department of Health** — www.doh.gov.uk
- **Medline-PubMed** — www.ncbi.nlm.nih.gov/PubMed (free system to search Medline)
- **National Association of Non-Principals** — www.nanp.org.uk
- **National Electronic Library for Health** — www.nelh.nhs.uk (primary care branch of NHS library)
- **NHS Centre for Evidence-Based Medicine** — www.cebm.net (evidence-based medicine information)
- **NHS Centre for Reviews and Dissemination** — www.york.ac.uk/inst/crd/ (effectiveness reviews for NHS)
- **NHS Information Authority** — www.nhsia.nhs.uk (NHS portal site)
- **Royal College of General Practitioners** — www.rcgp.org.uk
- **Royal College of Physicians** — www.rcplondon.ac.uk/index.asp
- **Royal College of Physicians of Edinburgh** — www.rcpe.ac.uk
- **West Midlands Deanery** — www.wmdeanery.org

Index